CW01512205

KINGSLEY L. DENNIS

IS THERE LIFE ON EARTH?

(The Transmutation Octave)

BEAUTIFUL TRAITOR BOOKS

Table of Contents

Introduction

The essays in this collection were written between February-April 2023. They were then left to hibernate, or ferment, for a year before being prepared for public release. Each essay represents movement through a musical octave – a cycle of transmutation. And within this transmutation sits humanity.

This essay cycle offers questioning, observations, commentary, analysis, speculations, and thought experiments regarding the current state of modern society, the human condition, possible future timelines, and potential cosmic scenarios. What can be said with some degree of certainty is that these essays are for the present times.

Humanity appears to be positioned within an arc of transmutation, with several potential permutations. However, the future may already have been actualized – upon some level – only that it has yet to manifest within the physical domain. And it is this manifestation or expression – this unfolding – that concerns us here. Humanity may already be poised upon the precipice or threshold, with only a little further to go. What awaits us, perhaps, is only a few nudges more …

Do

Beyond Materialism

*The human being has to become
what he thinks himself to be.*

~ Rudolf Steiner

We are having to adapt ourselves to a new loss – the demise of an old reality. Yet we should not mourn it but rather greet the new. There is no need to suffer in this readaptation; nor does it need to be overwhelming. Yet, there will be those needing recovery time. In modern terms, the world is going through an overhaul. When viewed through the metaphysical lens, it is a *transfiguration*. The human nervous system will be going through a vibrational recalibration; the mind will be rewiring its neuronal pathways; and a new orientation will be arising. Lucidity will come to replace the fog, eventually. As humankind passes through the current period of transmutation it is coming face-to-face with a moment, and an opportunity, for 'repentance.' Generally, people recognize 'repentance' from a religious standpoint – as in repentance for our sins – which signifies an atonement or penance. Yet the original etymology of the word comes from Greek, from *metanoiein*, what we now know as 'metanoia,' which means to change one's mind. It comes from *meta-noein*; literally, beyond 'nous,' or to think beyond. Repentance then – metanoia – is to change one's thinking and to shift consciousness by embracing thoughts beyond present limitations or current thought patterns. In this context, I propose we have entered a significant time for repentance – humanity, as a whole yet starting individually, needs to come through its current inertia in conscious thinking by altering how we comprehend matters and perceive our reality. And it is crucial that we do so, otherwise we shall find that a different way of thinking will overtake us and command humanity into a specific direction not to our future benefit.

For far too long, human cognition and perceptions have been constrained within a highly limited range and scope. Without exaggeration, there has been a densification and solidification of human thinking. It has literally been taken from creative heights (what some may refer to as 'flights of fancy') and become embedded into rock. This is the rock of materialism. The notion of metaphysical realities, the existence of events and sentience beyond the physical domain, has become diminished to the point of extinction. Why is this? Is it because humanity has suddenly become 'civilized'? I doubt this very much. In fact, I would be tempted to argue the opposite – that humanity is in contestation with forces that are acting against its civilizing impulse with deliberate intention. There are many groups (including occult groups, initiates, and elite circles) who are keen on spreading materialism and making arrangements to ensure that the majority of humanity believes only in materialism and are entirely under the influence of materialistic forces. As Steiner states: 'These initiates want to ensure that as many souls as possible only take in materialistic thoughts here between birth and death.' [1] Yet this form of materialism is not only in regard to our external habits, devices, and socio-cultural modes, but also (and most significantly) relating to a denial of all things 'of the spirit.' This refers to a wholesale agenda to establish a reality for humans that denies the existence of anything related to spirit, soul, and the metaphysical. This is nothing less than an imprisonment of spirit within the hard rock of materialism. We may even refer to this as a form of hyper-materialism. For some people, this may not seem so dangerous, or significant. After all, such things related to spirit and the metaphysical are just superstition anyway and have no place in a modern, technological world. This is not the place for fairies, djinns, demons, or angels. This is a world of physical reality, machines, and quantum computing. Ah, but you see, there is a contradiction here. Modern science, including technology, views the command and application of quantum capacities as the holy grail. And yet the quantum world itself is a realm of the supernatural. It is a realm of energy, and interrelation through time and space. It is an intermingling of the world of spirit (or consciousness-energy) into the world of matter. And since the quantum world is what underpins all physical manifestation – it is the underlying zero-point field of energy – then everything we know of in our physical reality is interspersed with the dimension of consciousness-spirit. Another way to put it is that everything that is sense perceptible is intermingled with the non-sense perceptible. The physical and the metaphysical are aspects of the same reality, depending on your scale of perception. Yet by only acknowledging one side of this we remain blind to the other. If we do not recognize, let alone understand, the metaphysical realm, then we cannot fully understand or appreciate the physical world. And this leaves us at a great disadvantage. Why is this so? It is because whoever understands how the metaphysical realm operates and intermingles (and thus influences) the physical realm will have the knowledge, and power, to manipulate the physical world to *their* advantage. By blocking out peoples' general awareness of the metaphysical by placing all attention and focus onto the physical, those aspects and influences beyond the general range of awareness can operate stealthily and undetected. This is why those aspects labelled as 'paranormal,' 'occult,' 'metaphysical,' and the rest, are ridiculed within mass culture. This is a diversion tactic to take away attention from anyone wishing to explore and develop further into the metaphysical. Because of this, those individuals and groups who have knowledge of how the metaphysical realm operates can continue, unabated and undisturbed, to apply that knowledge to establish events within the physical world that go largely unsuspected. Their dominion of control and influence over physical life continues unquestioned and uncontested. Rudolf Steiner recognized and spoke of this over one hundred years ago:

> ...something seemingly incomprehensible outwardly must indeed appear incomprehensible outwardly because there are spiritual forces and spiritual deeds being played out both for good and evil behind the scenes ... of events in world history.[2]

It is necessary at this time in humanity's growth to look beyond the 'scenery of existence' and to develop a general awareness not only of a metaphysical reality alongside the physical one, but also that these two realities are interlaced at all times – with the unseen, or non-sense perceptible, working through the physical world. It is counteractive for humanity to remain dormant in these regards at this particular time along its evolutionary transition. To remain steadfast within the thinking patterns and belief sets of a purely materialistic age will be damaging to its prospects for advancement. Some people may argue, of course, that it is exactly this materialistic age of ours that will steer humanity into a bright future through technological innovations as well as technological solutions to many of our current ills. The result of this perspective, however, will be a future along the lines of social technocracy and species transhumanism; with the consequences being the dissolution of the individual's connection with spirit-consciousness (the symbolic death of the spirit realms). Now is the time for humanity to be guided more in accordance with metaphysical – or esoteric, transcendental principles – than ever before; otherwise, greater concentrations of power will be in the hands of fewer and fewer people who will exercise this control over the masses in a negative way. The struggle that is currently playing out is through certain groups (and agendas) striving to develop a cultural environment of hyper-materialism that will paralyse, or at the very least impede, the human being's perceptive development. Anything related to the 'unseen' – and this includes consciousness – will be regarded as whimsy, nonsense, and as fantasy, to the point that all aspects relating to anything remotely metaphysical will be rejected outright as belonging to an archaic time. Even now it can be seen that people are being inoculated, metaphorically speaking, against the inclination to perceive metaphysical promptings, resulting in them losing any urge for a genuine spiritual life, or inner development.

The forces of materialism (what I have previously called *entropic forces*) are operative within most of our societies, and upon the world stage, and their aim is to confuse the general masses and to steer them into believing what is being shown to them. It is a grand psychological operation as much as it is occult, for it operates on several levels simultaneously and only the outer shards are visible. In the determination to steer humanity away from metaphysical truths, these forces are attempting to overwhelm our senses and emotions, and to herd the collective into states of fear, insecurity, and dependency. These stressful states then align the individual to a lower frequency that connects (or entrains) people to a denser vibratory rate. To become entangled within these denser, lower vibrations leads to a diminishing connection to finer, metaphysical impulses, which results in the erosion of the inner, developmental urge. As I put forth here, it is necessary for human beings to establish a correct relationship with the spiritual/metaphysical reality. Never before has this been so necessary for us. It can be said that this is now as necessary as choosing what we consume for the health of the body.

We need to be extra vigilant and alert now to how events are unfolding upon the physical plane – especially upon the world stage – and to take note of those things that attract our attention; and to notice how things are being revealed to us through mainstream channels. We should be mindful of such impacts and to question why they are attempting to influence certain reactions and responses. The thoughts, emotions, and reactions that we produce serve to make us in their image. As the opening citation to this essay reminds us, we are to become what we think ourselves to be – and not to become in the image that others are portraying for us. How we think, and the manner in which we convey these thoughts, is generally overlooked and not recognized to have any great significance. Yet this is not the case. If we remember – *In the beginning was the Word.* The power of the word, and the thought behind it, is seen nowadays as a casual and almost abstract thing. Rather than being recognized as a real force, the power of the word has been turned into Twitterings, emojis, and abbreviated tick-tockering mutterings. Our modern societies have curtailed and corrupted the power of thought. Human expression has been swiftly, and cleverly, replaced by abstract, disjointed thoughts and communications, supported by media programming, entertainment, and the rest. The masses have been tech-herded into corrals dominated by quick videos, viral memes, comedy skits, and (yes, I have to say it) cute cats. It is a fairground that celebrates the death of spirit-consciousness. Yet it is a death only by absence and not in reality. At all times, the impulse of spirit-consciousness moves about and through the physical world, unknown to and unsuspected by the majority. Yet just because we are unaware of it does not deny its existence. You may close your eyes to block the sun, yet this does nothing to deny the existence and influence of the sun. The point here, however, is that if people remain unaware of these factors, then these forces or impulses remain within the collective unconscious. It is now central to our epoch that as many individuals as possible become perceptive to the conscious and metaphysical forces/energies that lie beyond the threshold of aware consciousness.

Conscious awareness of events and impulses that lie beyond our normal ken of perception help us to recognize the action and influence of negating or counteractive forces. I would propose that in these times it is the responsibility of humanity to 'come to grips with evil as an impulse in world evolution.'[3] For if we are aware of the influence of these intervening and disruptive agencies, then we can begin to dissolve them of their power through, firstly, the recognition and acknowledgement of their existence. As it was written in the Gnostic Gospel of Philip: 'So long as the root of wickedness is hidden, it is strong. But when it is recognized, it is dissolved. When it is revealed, it perishes … It is powerful because we have not recognized it.' The responsibility for us right now is a difficult yet necessary one: it is for us to recognize and confront these negative, counteractive forces and to bring them into the light (literally and metaphorically). The severest hindrance to this is only our collective ignorance. And yet we need to also recognize that metaphysical forces are always aligned with our intentions for growth and perceptual advancement. The very reason that certain power-hungry groups aim to cause as much confusion, distraction, and dissonance as possible amongst human life is to obscure these metaphysical impulses from our awareness and to, quite literally, keep us in the dark. They fear our growing awareness – and it *is* growing amongst the general populace. It is necessary for individuals to awaken through their own compulsion. It is time for a grand recognition and revealing. And this changing of our minds (our perceptions) is the great moment of repentance – metanoia – signifying the shift in consciousness by embracing perceptive awareness beyond present limitations.

Humanity's great defence is not through physical means but by knowledge. If we know about such things, we can be protected from them. Yet we should not be lazy in seeking out real knowledge of these things. We should not be deterred by false-flag events or false promises. Neither should we be misdirected by false information and accusations. When the finger points outwards, we should look inward and to the heart (and ignore the narrated script). The real power we have is through what we know, and therefore what we are able to think. We would do well to remember that we become what we think. And we each now are being called to become that which we are truly able to think, to know, and to be.

References

[1] Steiner, R. (2006) *Secret Brotherhoods and the Mystery of the Human Double*. Forest Row: Rudolf Steiner Press, p135

[2] Steiner, R. (2006) *Secret Brotherhoods and the Mystery of the Human Double*. Forest Row: Rudolf Steiner Press, p78

[3] Steiner, R. (2006) *Secret Brotherhoods and the Mystery of the Human Double*. Forest Row: Rudolf Steiner Press, p162

Shock One

The Raising of Conscious Energy

To all intents and purposes, it would seem that humanity, life on this planet, and the planet itself, have a timeline in which to accomplish evolutionary goals in alignment with larger cosmic cycles. According to various investigations into earth cataclysms, there are regular intervals where great upheaval is experienced upon the earth, often accompanied by a magnetic reversal – or what is generally referred to as a 'pole flip.' These geomagnetic reversals are said to be related to when our solar system passes through a particular portion of galactic space. One perspective is that there are regions of extremely low magnetic fields – sometimes called *null zones* – that precede geomagnetic reversals. Another perspective, gaining popularity, is that around every 12,000 years or so our solar system passes through an energized portion of galactic space known as the 'galactic rift' or 'galactic sheet.' This zone of heightened energy is a catalyst for triggering these periodic pole shifts upon the earth. These are very brief allusions to various forms of cataclysmic perspectives. What can be proposed, without little doubt, is that the earth goes through periods of relative calm (cosmically speaking), interspersed with cyclical interventions that bring great upheaval. Within these periods of 'relative calm,' which span in thousands of years in human-earth time (such as 12,000 years), various human civilizations rise and fall, and the human species has the opportunity to reach particular evolutionary goals. Presumably, these evolutionary goals for the human species are then either reset (repeated or transcended) after a cosmic intervention of great upheaval. There is reason to suppose that within the last one thousand years especially, there have been efforts to assist in the raising of human consciousness to a greater level than previously during this particular window of 'cosmic opportunity.'

It can be surmised that there was a plan to raise the conscious energy of the West, for example, in line with a specific timeline. A certain modicum of information and knowledge had to be made available for people to have access to materials suited to their own mental development. Also, preparation had to have begun in order to lay the groundwork for later actualization – or a 'switching on' of a new consciousness frequency. If we take just a cursory glance at history, it can be seen how the initiate path and ancient knowledge in past times was heavily guarded and very seldom were its secrets channelled into the public domain. Initiate operations were carried out behind the scenes of everyday life or released in ways not recognizable to the masses. Such operations in past epochs that were released into the social currents of life have included the Troubadour movement, the Grail Quest, the Tarot, alchemy, Cabbalah, and others. Yet from the middle of the 19th century, from around 1850 onwards, there seems to have been a decision taken to release a stream of knowledge from the wisdom traditions into the public domain. This began with the rise of spiritualism that then led to Theosophy, Anthroposophy, occult traditions (e.g., the Golden Dawn), the Gurdjieff Work, and others. Also, from the early to mid-20th century, knowledge and wisdom from the East arrived upon western shores and many Teachers were sent to the West to prepare the psychology and mental reception of people in this hemisphere. Why did this grand operation suddenly appear – and what were its aims?

At the end of each developmental epoch, humanity receives energy in order to activate a new organ necessary for the incoming epoch. This new organ is required to receive the conscious energy that will be part of the future era. This energy is always made available as the incumbent era is in decline. Each new developmental organ within humanity allows for it to receive a wider spectrum of metaphysical reality. This, naturally, antagonizes those forces that are intent on maintaining their current power regime. For this reason, there tends to be a counter-initiative established by certain 'ruling forces' to block the incoming energies and to impede the general masses in the reception of aforesaid energies. At each particular epoch there is a scale of perception, or spectrum of awareness, which is dominant. At each given transition to a new developmental era for humankind, the 'organ of perception' is further activated so that there is greater access to, and comprehension of, metaphysical realities beyond the current scale. It may be that in our time now, organs of perceptive clairvoyance and telepathy are due for activation within humankind. This is evidenced by this faculty already being present (activated) within a small percentage of humankind. At each stage, there are forerunners within the general populace who display the new developmental faculties. In earlier times, such people were ostracized, heavily persecuted, or even killed, for showing such capacities. Such myths and folklore around witches, sorcerers, seers, and sages come to mind in this regard. There is always a precursor wave of people displaying the properties of the new developmental organ prior to a more widespread activation as the new epoch comes closer within the timeline. In each stage of human history there have been superstitions regarding such people, or the presence of such abilities, and yet in later times people look back upon these superstitions and laugh at their 'primitive' nature. Also, as people in past times did not have the capacities to access direct spiritual truths, and because it is a natural law that spiritual truths must be always made available to people, such wisdom was placed into human cultures through the way of myths, stories, legends, folklore and fairy tales, etc. Cultural dissemination of metaphysical knowledge thus had to be made via particular mediums or vehicles that were either co-opted or established specifically for these means. Again, such vehicles as the Cabbala, occultism, ceremonial magic, esoteric schools, etc., can be seen as transmissions of metaphysical knowledge, alongside others that took a more indirect path and may have emerged as cultural events and artistic movements.

It also happens that within the transitional period there is increased social and cultural friction, for such energetics may assist in the activation of the developmental organs. As Jalāl al-Dīn Rumi stated as far back as the 13th century: '*New organs of perception come into being as a result of necessity. Therefore, O man, increase your necessity, so that you may increase your perception.*' There will be those people who are able to create the necessity by a force of will (inner drive) yet for the majority of people an external event or series of impacts ('chaotic attractors') may be required. It is these external impacts that frequently cause friction and upheaval, yet their presence is necessary, albeit unrecognized by most people at the time. Transitions between significant epochs within the life of humanity are thus often viewed as turbulent; and this is generally considered to be due to random or purely physical events with no metaphysical intention behind them. At the same time, there is always a portion of the populace who are unable to pass the 'threshold of the epoch' in terms of aligning with the frequencies of the incoming developmental impulse. This segment of society may then enter a path of devolvement for the remainder of the epoch as they have left the stream of evolutionary humanity. This process may be referred to as passing, or not, the *threshold of initiation.* Such a threshold could occur in alignment with a timeframe of cyclical catastrophe, as discussed above. It may well be said that a successful passing of the threshold entails entering upon a different frequency of reality, and thus consciousness. This shift to a developmental frequency (sometimes referred to as transcendence), allows for a segment of humanity to further the evolutionary goals of the species upon the new level. This necessity to pass the threshold might also occur around the same time as a catastrophic geological upheaval (from cosmic origins) yet not always. Either way, it is a time for intense active work.

The approach to such 'thresholds' within the overall transmutation octave can be said to be a time for immense 'soul making' and great activity on the part of the metaphysical impulse. It might also be framed in the context of reaping the most benefits within the timeframe available (the harvest) before the fields are to be burnt and sowed for renewal. At the same time, such chaotic periods are when the metaphysical impulse appears most absent and/or is a time of socio-cultural disarray. British historian Arnold Toynbee who, from his extensive meta-historical study on the rise and fall of civilizations, came up with his 'Law of Progressive Simplification.' By this, Toynbee indicated that civilizational growth was not so much measured by material resources but rather by its ability to transfer increasing amounts of energy and attention towards non-material growth, such as creativity, wellbeing, the inner life, etc. Toynbee also coined the term 'etherealization' to describe the historical process whereby a society learns to accomplish the same, or more, using less time and energy. This period of etherealization suggests a focus on metaphysical pursuits at the expense of deepening materialism. However, when materialistic pursuit becomes the overriding and dominant focus then this suggests a downturn into a period of civilizational decline. Such decline may also, at times, be aligned with both larger civilizational and geological periods at the end of a great cycle. Another British historian, Nicholas Hagger, has examined the last 5,000 years of world history and charted the rise and fall of 25 major civilizations that, he says, grew around a metaphysical Light/Fire impulse before declining. In his monumental work *The Fire and the Stones*, Hagger outlines how civilizations pass through 61 secularizing stages.[1] He examines how the metaphysical Fire/Light sustains a civilization to its peak, and when this impulse fades or is withdrawn, the civilization goes into decline and eventual decay as the Fire/Light is extinguished. These instances where the metaphysical impulse emerges can be regarded as operations – injections or transmissions – of conscious energies in a bid to raise the general conscious energy of certain peoples and communities at particular times and places across the planet during the larger arc between grander cyclic renewals.

Even a cursory glance throughout the annals of history shows a vast dispersal and transmission of esoteric and mystical doctrines and teachings from a seemingly endless array of learned figures; some of whom have appeared to act in odd circumstances and through almost inspired behaviours. There is certainly no shortage of mystics, sages, and both direct and indirect teachers of what we may call the *metaphysical fire*. History is littered with the names of many of these messengers; although we can also surmise there would have been many more messengers or 'transmitters' that acted unseen and outside of the spotlight of recognition. Although the 'wisdom stream,' as it is referred to, is said to have been, and continues to be, present at all times throughout human history, there are periods of greater activity as well as fallow periods where the wisdom operations take a step back from public life. It would seem fair to say, considering the external circumstances of the present age, that humanity has entered a time of intense activity upon the metaphysical plane. This suggests that interventions and operations of the transcendental impulse – the *metaphysical fire* – have entered a heightened phase at this specific period, with perhaps a noticeable focus upon the West.

The twenty-first century started dramatically, and quite literally, with grand explosions, and rather than ceasing or decelerating has in fact been accelerating along these trends. Alongside external geopolitical circumstances, the so-called modern world has quickened its rush into materialism to a point where we may consider the situation as being hyper-materialist. Such an environment has been less than conducive to religio-spiritual ideals; on the contrary, a deep secularism has progressed parallel, or even intrinsic to, the march of materialism. In this context, the presence of mystics, sages, and spiritual teachers has been ambiguous. It would appear that these have split into several avenues: i) they are ridiculed by mass society and/or seen as relics of a past era; ii) they are viewed as exotic or oriental icons that attract the curiosity seekers; or, iii) rogue individuals and groups have set themselves up to commercially gain from the demand of such mystique.

A genuine wisdom source is likely, in most circumstances, to have stepped back from the mode/role of the outwardly 'Spiritual Teacher' some time ago. Certainly, in the West at least, the 'oriental identity' style of wisdom transmission would now be considered a non-operational mode by genuine sources. If such schools/groupings exist then they are more than likely to be the traces or residues of earlier, original impulses that are now perpetuated through static structures. The metaphysical impulse for the current period would most probably choose a medium most in-keeping with the milieu of its time. The question remains, however: what would such mediums be, and how could we recognize them?

What can be surmised from all this is that there will be various forms of the metaphysical impulse operating throughout diverse human cultures across the globe. Many, if not all, of these will go unnoticed by most people. This is partly because so few individuals are seeking for access to a genuine developmental impulse. As it is generally known, people attract those things in accordance with their own state of being and vibrational frequency. In order to attract the energetics of a developmental impulse, an individual must first do some of the work. And this requires a minimal amount of effort and focus. Resonant attraction is a two-way process; that is, there must be that which attracts and that which receives, and both elements are required. The essence of the human being is of the same substance from which it is originally derived (it's Source). Hence, it retains the same *vibratory signature* and is naturally attracted to its counterpart. Resonant attraction does not get abolished by distance – the further away the parts are – yet its strength of attraction can become vastly diminished. The dense materialism of our times, coupled with a heavy, terrestrial, somewhat telluric, consciousness, has obscured the signal (the 'attraction') from getting through. The metaphysical impulse therefore requires that there is a greater lightness upon the waters of this planetary sphere. It is time for the coal within the coalmine to become as diamonds; and this requires a degree of crushing of the carbon. It may be surmised then that humanity is now passing through a phase of increased pressure – of chaotic nodes and catalysts – as an accelerated means to form diamonds within the carbon life of the human being.

References

[1] Hagger, Nicholas (1991) *The Fire and the Stones.* Dorset: Element Books.

Si

Chaotic Nodes & Catalysts
(forces of decline & order)

*'What is old and outlived is not willing to give way, and
tries to prolong its anachronistic
existence by various illegitimate means. Thus
destructive forces arise within civilization and culture;
forces of decline and disintegration.'*

~ G.A. Bondarev

It comes as no surprise to learn that there are forces and players that wish to place the entire earth, and global human civilization, under the domination of materialism. And the character of the Anglo-American nations are perhaps better suited to be the front wave in this process. The forerunners in the promotion and implementation of deep materialism will come from these so-called 'developed western nations.' They shall serve as a prototype for the transformation of human society into a realm of deeply embedded techno-materialism. To execute this process, many high-profile people are sought out (such as politicians, financiers, and celebrities) to be the puppets – the *marionettes* – for promoting this agenda. This is the present state of affairs, regardless of how things may appear upon the shimmering surface. We have arrived upon a defining threshold that will dictate how people will proceed in their life experience upon this planet. How each person decides to pass this threshold will depend upon the choices and decisions they take now and within the proceeding years. As such a threshold approaches in the life of any human society or civilization, greater forces of chaos are unleashed at the same time there is the necessity for a drive towards coherent order. It is the ordering principle that allows a successful crossing of the transformational threshold whilst the chaotic attractor propels people, agencies, bodies, etc, into a distracting path away from the threshold and into an evolutionary dead-end.

Within the previous phase of human civilization, a life of the senses became the defining impulse, with emphasis upon the external, physical aspects. Around the middle to late 19th century a new impulse was introduced into modern western life that had as its aim the familiarization with non-physical realms of reality. This was the beginning of the spiritualism movement, alongside early American transcendentalism, theosophy, and occult themes which were to signal the beginning of a metaphysical impulse to prepare human society for the coming transformational period. Up until this time, human civilization had been immersed in a period of dense physicality and the growth of the individual. There had been a turning away from the metaphysical life, and at the same time many social forces were working to keep the transcendental impulse out of human life. This impulse had been replaced by an earthly static-religious structure based on rigid protocols rather than inspiration from the inner life. The physical life experience had become one of material content rather than metaphysical exploration. It was coming to a point where it was almost impossible for human culture as a collective to take up the spiritual impulse. This coincided with the explosion of the second industrial revolution and the workhouses for the poor. Spiritual pursuits were a phantasmagorical luxury that few could afford. This situation was dramatically counteracted by the introduction of spiritualism, seances, afterlife phenomena, and eventually the appearance of the 'Hidden Masters' into human affairs. For all the controversy against Theosophy and the figures of Helena Blavatsky, Colonel Henry Steel Olcott, and later Annie Besant, the movement had the effect of seeding a new stream of metaphysical ideas and teachings into the modern western era. As mentioned in the preceding essay, this literally opened the floodgates to a flow of personages that arrived upon the new shores promulgating occult, esoteric, and metaphysical teachings. The list is very, very long; and the ground, it seemed, was incredibly fertile. Yet where there is a visible intervention of such forces, they almost certainly attract their counterparts of the denying or negating forces.

As in a game, there are forces seeking to maintain balance and development and those with the aim to disrupt the balance. On the micro level, some of these forces can be recognized as individuals, groups, and organizations. On the macro level, these forces are not to be personified or anthropomorphized (i.e., humanized as specific personalities). Some forces can be recognized as supporting processes of disembodied fantasy; others as pushing for domination of intellect and deep materialism. However, without forces of opposition there would be no true or genuine freedom. The human agency of willpower needs to be exercised and strengthened, and this is accomplished through making choices and decisions, and acting upon them. Without friction there would be no movement – only *the illusion of movement*. Therefore, there are forces that can be utilized to develop a person's own development even if these same forces are acting out of their own selfish, and even conflictual, interests. Without the ability to make a choice, the human being becomes a mere automaton. Until we face that dreadful moment (of being a human automaton) we have the challenge to pursue the path of human development through our responses to the counterforces that are blocking human advancement. And this challenge, far from disempowering us, has the opportunity to compel us even greater. These opportunities are what I refer to as the *chaotic catalysts*. And it appears that some of these 'chaotic catalysts' are now very active upon a global level.

A part of our human freedom to choose includes the ability to choose disbelief. What we choose not to believe forms as much of our condition as those things we do choose to believe. In this, certain forces of negation have their function, and it assists us to recognize this. It is within such times as these, of negating forces vying for dominance, that the urge of the metaphysical impulse can be felt by those who are receptive to it. The greater the physical disturbances, the more the metaphysical impulse is sensed in its need to infuse the material life. During moments of condensed, and intense, transformational periods within human evolution, there is likewise an increase in those 'hindering forces' that seek to contest the developmental surge. In such times, these disruptive forces increase their presence and interventions in an attempt to hamper, or block, the influence of the subtle forces within the earthly life of humankind. At the same time, it can be said that these 'chaotic catalysts' help to make available a period of transformational opportunity through providing disruptions that are more visible and thus actionable. It also marks a time, for those people receptive to influences of spirit-consciousness, to become more aware, alert, and proactively responsive to these impulses. As the transmutation octave comes near to the end of one of its cycles, there is inevitably a greater release of forces – affirming and denying – into the physical dimension. It becomes paramount for the individual to activate the power of human discernment and the choice to seek out order – inner balance and equilibrium – for this will create the necessary vibrational signature (resonance). Because of this, the forces of chaos are strongest in these areas, and seek to diminish balance and order by the most pervasive and intrusive means possible. Within this period of deep materialism (or *hyper-materialism*), these intrusive means are brought forward through the use of dominant technologies that monitor, track, and regulate human behaviour. Biological forms of social management are to be transferred into artificial structures and arrangements, presided over by machinic, programmed intelligence networks.

The counter-balancing task (the establishment of order) is for those people with receptive capacity to prepare themselves for the infusion of spirit-consciousness (the *metaphysical fire*) into the physical, and to become as receivers-transmitters for these energies. This requires that a person not only be balanced – bodily, mentally, and emotionally – but also to not be vibrationally entangled with the lower frequencies of dissonance that increasingly plague the physical domain. The alignments with spirit-consciousness are to be more subtle and less visible in outward form. The age of 'identifiable worship,' such as through external rituals, dress codes, and other exterior signs of belonging, are to be replaced by a non-dramatized, quiet, and almost unnoticeable inward alignment. The days of external spiritual form have passed. The living spirit is now to carried quietly, and with dignity, within the human vessel. This is the merger that brings life on earth closer to the spiritualization of matter. The new epoch we are moving into is not one that is to be defined through outer forms but through inward fluidity. This is the Quiet Path.

The intelligence needed now within humankind is one that grasps not the dry intellect but steers inner thoughts towards development of the spirit-consciousness. Intelligence is not something a person *has* but rather something they *use*. And the question revolves around how these uses are employed. A person of negative intent can be extremely intelligent and use this for destructive or damaging purposes. The energy of consciousness can be utilized in various ways. Humanity are the vessels for the employment of universal energies, and it would serve us well to recognize this. That is why we are seeing now a huge push for the implementation of AI (machinic intellect) as this opens up a different evolutionary stream and possibilities – possibilities that deny the expansion of human intelligence through spirit-consciousness. However, to not recognize, or acknowledge, that metaphysical events are in operation around us at all times, only gives sustenance to the 'hardening effect' of materialism and the entropic forces. It is this *hardening* within modern life that we must be particularly aware of. This process affects the senses, the perceptive faculties, and the sensitivity to receptivity. An energetic, vibrational hardening or densification, so to speak, creates a blockage for contact with developmental impulses. This is where the path of human will and free choice comes in.

The path of free choice brings with it the responsibility to make those choices. Free choice also means that an individual has the freedom to choose to align with the darker elements, as well as choosing to serve the developmental forces. There may be greater risks in this degree of flexibility, yet choosing to serve without being compelled also accelerates the impulses of development. As it is said, freedom without choice is meaningless. With every step taken towards freedom, a person also gets closer to the darker aspects, for they must be confronted, and a choice made (known as the *temptation*). The more a person follows the path of freedom, the more they will be confronted with the 'temptations.' And by choosing against the temptations (or darker aspects), so is the freedom more whole and complete. The very presence of the entropic, chaotic counterforces gives the choice to align with the path of evolvement greater weight. In other words, the choice of freedom is its fullest when chosen against an opposition to it. Each new temptation can serve to strengthen the presence of spirit-consciousness according to the choices and actions made. Without opposition, a choice carries less weight. And life, we are constantly reminded, does not take place within a vacuum. If this has not been fully appreciated before, then now is certainly the time for its realization. As Rudolf Steiner said in 1908:

> The good would not be so great a good if it were not to grow through the conquest of evil. Love would not be so intense if it had not to become love so great as to be able even to overcome the wickedness in the countenance of evil men …

> You must not think that evil has no part in the
> plan of creation. It is there in order that through
> it may come the greater good.[1]

Life is an amalgam of forces, and their interplay
through creation and destruction – order and chaos –
creates form and movement. By having the choice of
movement, we also accept the responsibility of having to
leave things behind once their time is done. Furthermore,
momentum requires friction (again, the absence of a
vacuum). It is because so few people have the awareness
of such processes that there exists a meta-history of those
events and processes that have been operating behind the
scenes of everyday life. What we generally know of as
history, as socio-cultural life, is the shaking of the leaves;
what we are unaware of is the wind that blows through the
tree.

The entropic, chaotic forces understand the laws of
evolutionary development, which means that they cannot
oppose them directly but instead they have to move within
these currents and try to distort them – to give them a
wrong direction, to slow them down or speed them up.
That is why we have deception, hidden power, and
trickery within our systems as these are the means
whereby such forces can project their influence and
manifest their power. Yet they cannot act directly, for to

do so would be against natural universal laws. They act through duplicity. And, in general, people validate such actions and events through sheer ignorance of the deceit enacted against them. Often, this ignorance is solidified by attachments to lower sensory impacts, influences, and desires. The human is capable of developing their higher faculties through overcoming lower sensate attachments. Some of the people who unleash great tragedies are influenced by occult forces; they bear this responsibility. Likewise, those individuals capable of aligning with positive, constructive metaphysical forces must also bear this responsibility. However, a distinction in these positions should be made. We should desist from 'doing battle' with such negating forces in our physical life, for then we are engaging with them on their playing field – on their energetic level. Beyond the physical, there are 'events' taking place unknown to us (the metaphysical forces are aware of the darker occult forces). For us, the responsibility is to gain awareness of the environment in which we are developing the human condition. Human beings do not exist in a neutral environment. Having awareness of those impulses and influences that constitute this environment is critical if we are to have a clarity of perception. Yet being aware of such things does not mean that we need to engage with them. In many instances, we are to observe and, if possible, gain insight into how such interventions and negating influences attempt to sway us. As Rudolf Steiner states: 'If only enough people would have the impulse today to say: we have first of all to gain insight into these things, the rest will follow!'[2] What is necessary is to cultivate a *right relation* to the things of this manifested world.

Our regular senses are unable to penetrate very far beyond external appearances. That is why people live within a surface, or superficial, layer of experience. And this layer is very deceiving for it is being continuously penetrated by those forces and influences beyond physical perception. The vying forces of chaos and order are not recognized for what they are. Instead, such aspects are often misrepresented as being either 'good' or 'bad' despite the necessity for such forces to push and pull against one another. Too much of one, and there would be stillness, inertia, and stagnation. Too much of the other, and there would be uncontrolled fluidity and fluctuation. There needs to be a blending. As the mystic-philosopher Gurdjieff said: 'The higher blends with the lower to actualize the middle.' Most people are unaware of how these forces operate, let alone that they exist as they do within manifested reality. For this reason, individuals can benefit from acquiring a degree of self-knowledge; otherwise, those with the capacity to comprehend the forces of chaos and order will be driven by outer impulses that they are internally unaware of. The transmutation that faces humankind offers a great potential for moving ahead upon the celestial arc, where the forces of chaos and order play their part for the benefit of evolutionary goals. The more that humanity steps forward upon this path, the more is learnt and understood about the cosmic playing field that constitutes the arena of our lives.

References

[1] Rudolf Steiner, a lecture from June 25th, 1908 (GA 104) https://rsarchive.org/Lectures/GA104/English/APC1958/ 19080625p01.html

[2] Rudolf Steiner, a lecture from December 12th, 1918 (GA 186) - https://rsarchive.org/Lectures/19181212p01.html

La

The Divergent Forces of Neo-Nihilism

'Yes, the world is an illusion. But Truth is always being shown there.'

~ Idries Shah, The Dermis Probe.

A world of appearances has been in the making for a long time; much longer than the passing zeitgeists of various ideologies. Only that in each age, such appearances take on designated forms. And yet the more detached from reality is the age, the greater is the sense of abstractness, and thus meaninglessness or nihilism. The spectre of nihilism is but the head of a larger creature that represents a broader state of the human condition. The historian Oswald Spengler noted that nihilism begins when the vulgar rises and becomes more widespread than the decent elements in society. Spengler also famously announced a century ago that the Western world is ending, and we are witnessing the final season – the 'winter' – of its civilizational decline. If we are to believe Spengler, then the western world has been in decline for a solid one hundred years now. And yet, for many people, the world has never seemed more satisfying, with access to so much more content-rich lifestyles and social satisfiers. Yet, perhaps it is more the case that over the last decades, just enough of a trickle of meaning and purpose was provided by worldly living so that the spectre of meaninglessness has been kept at bay. Now, however, it would seem that the natives are becoming restless. And not just the natives of the West are becoming restless, but globally. Spengler may have been correct in surmising that the western world has been in decline for the past century or more; certainly, in our current times, the geo-political Western block is fast losing its power base. Yet it seems apparent that something larger is in operation – a cyclic decline, perhaps? There is certainly an energetic shift noticeable across the planet, with increased dissonance, unease, anxiety, trauma, depression, nervousness, and more. Some of these conditions could be put down to a correspondence in the Earth's decreasing magnetic fields and the increasing influx of solar and cosmic radiation. However, a grander psychic imbalance is in play through humanity's collective psychology, and questions of meaning and purpose are arising.

The English philosopher Colin Wilson believed that modern existentialism – the alienation, nihilism, and boredom of modern life – results from a 'fallacy of insignificance.' In other words, a feeling that the human being is nothing, and has no role or true place in the world.[1] Further, that the human sense of insignificance is not only a grand fallacy but that it is being promoted by increased materialism – and what I will later refer to as *dark materialism*. Yet matters have changed dramatically in the world since Wilson produced his prognosis more than fifty years ago. Recently, Israeli historian Yuval Noah Harari has been announcing that the immediate future holds little hope for a new underclass of 'irrelevant' and 'useless' people. In previous centuries, says Harari, people revolted against exploitation, oppression, tyranny, etc; now, they fear becoming irrelevant.[2] Huge numbers of individuals will find themselves living in a society that doesn't need them anymore. It is a harder battle to struggle against irrelevance as there is nothing tangible to cling to or to reassure you against the encroaching insignificance other than your inner or innate sense of self. This leads to a psychological state of nihilism, for nihilism is ultimately a question of truth – a truth about oneself and how a person feels themselves to be within the experience of physical life.

Our external lives are filled with reams of relative truths; from scientific, to religious and the philosophic. Modern life has shifted from a position of overarching systemic 'educated objectivities' to a splattering of individual subjectivities. Whatever truths were peddled as part of the pre-existing consensus narratives (Religion, Science, etc.,) are undergoing a vast refurbishment whilst their replacements do not seem to be arriving any time soon. Almost every aspect of modern life has become questionable. Scepticism and disbelief (or non-belief) has replaced much of our civilizational questioning. Internal questioning has been substituted with a new form of cultural obedience – internal persuasion from without. When all major global, governmental, and human management systems are founded on untruths and blatant misconceptions, then the problem stems from the core of the system itself and infuses outwards into the people. Deception is the blood of the current cultural beast. Within such a system, the only end to nihilism is tyranny and totalitarianism. Any revolution born out of apathy and existential angst will only feed the false Kingdom of this world. It has happened before. Tyrannical regimes such as Fascism and National Socialism exploited the sense of restlessness to feed into their own purposes and agenda of authoritarianism. It is because nihilism produces, or is produced from, an inner disquiet that people become unmoored from their grounding, start to drift, and are then much more susceptible to forces of mass formation and false solidarity (as so clearly shown by the work of psychologist Mattias Desmet). Furthermore, this itching sense of disquiet is often covered up through the seeking of activities and distractions that provide a temporary sense of well-being. This is the opportune time for certain pseudo-spiritualities – or 'new spiritualities' – to claim a sway of new clients. It is a time for magicians dressed in robes of quantum entanglement to proclaim the oneness and 'cosmic connectivity' of all. Anything to escape from the restlessness and meaninglessness of a materially empty existence. According to Seraphim Rose, the spectre of nihilism has already arrived at our shores:

> ... Nihilism has become, in our time, so widespread and pervasive, has entered so thoroughly and so deeply into the minds and hearts of all men living today, that there is no longer any "front" on which it may be fought; and those who think they are fighting it are most often using its own weapons, which they in effect turn against themselves.[3]

This nihilism has become pervasive because there is no longer any relationship – either tangible or non-tangible – to even relative truths. The religious, spiritual, cultural (even political) ropes of attachment have become irretrievably severed. The only hope that has been offered in the place of the void is technological – a techno-materialism promoted as the machine of ultimate progress. The artificial construct is being praised as the 'new authenticity.' As philosopher Walter Benjamin would say, we now live within the age/cage of mechanical reproduction. There is no desire or wish for a return to the old authority systems. There is a fast grab for the replacement; and within this void of desperation, people will be almost willing for a new 'great reset.'

The deepening materialism of the digital age/cage is constructing a false playground out of the increased dismantling of all the prior structures of morality and ordered meanings. The pandemic and post-pandemic pressure forced more and more people into online and digital lifestyles. The rising management systems of the carbon-controlled 'green economy' will further establish an architecture of monitored and curated needs. This emerging architecture of control is what I have referred to as the 'machinic impulse' and it takes the pre-existing forms of nihilism to a new level. The nihilism that existed prior to our current times was a rejection of moral and/or religious principles, and a feeling or philosophical perspective that nothing in the world has a real existence or meaning. However, our consensus reality has been and continues to be manipulated so the 'normal' state of affairs is now a world of deep fakes, post-truth, and narrative manipulation until we are not sure if 'the world has a real existence' at the best of times. The nihilism that the encroaching era of deep materialism is creating is what can be called as *neo-nihilism*. Neo-nihilism can be viewed as constant uncertainty and untruths disguised as knowledge when it is nothing more than a power-control structure. This neo-nihilism is, I would posit, a loss of meaning and reality-grounding through a new technological world order that strips a person of any sense of inner being and triggers various unseen neuroses. Psychoanalysis tells us that neurosis is part of the humanization process – the limitation of experience; the fragmentation of perception; the dispossession of internal control. In other words, it is a 'falling away from one's being' – a de-centeredness – a lack of a moral-spirit centre. This inner void creates disorientation. It is not a social-cultural or a political nihilism but a psychological one. It is a denial and (dis)belief centred around the same thing – a nothingness or zero-space. Out of this zero-space may arise a techno-mediated world of the absurd – a machinic rationality that becomes the new irrational form of narrative. This new 'irrational narrative' would have the aim of becoming the next form of world structure. However, it is necessary first to dismantle the old

53

narratives that held the old order together. In terms of a power structure, it would be better to crush the old narratives so that their remnants do not try to rise up to confront the new programming. This was seen with the National Socialism of the Nazis: it wasn't only a physical new order but also, importantly, a psychological one. The new order must dethrone its imagined enemies to declare a new security state, or world order of security.

A new form of organization is coming into existence that represents this neo-nihilistic era of the dying cultural age. It represents a kind of lucid absurdity where technique and precision are paramount and displays an appalling insensitivity toward the human and the 'being' of humanity. This neo-nihilist form of organization corresponds to a terraforming and transformation of the earth and society by machines, artificial intelligence, and the inhuman ideology of social management and engineering that accompanies it. Its aim is to become a highly centralized power regime that consumes all forms of knowledge and truth divergent to its own ideological narratives: 'For if there is no truth, power knows no limit save that imposed by the medium in which it functions, or by a stronger power opposed to it.'[4] The ideological narrative, from the neo-nihilist power structure's point of view, will be one of perfect rationality and technological progress that provides for a world of total liberation. Yet it shall be a materialist's pseudo-utopia for, in truth, it will be the vastest, and most efficient, digital iron cage humans have ever known – for it will be pervasive and untouchable. Yet this is not the most worrying issue. The more disturbing aspect here is that there is a power-drive to establish the organization for a 'new earth' that is opposed to the cyclic evolutionary impulses. The core object of this project is for a transformation of humankind into a new planetary species body. It shall be a planetary species greatly reduced in number and highly segregated by status and servitude. And most importantly, it will be based on a collective humanized mass that functions at a lower vibration of being and self. In other words, a great planetary change is coming to the Earth as the planet – and human civilization – transits from one cycle into another. And a small number of wealthy and powerful individuals, with immense hubris, are attempting to manage and steer this transition to favour their materialistic goals at the expense of the many.

At the end of a grand cycle there is generally a sense of psychic malaise as well as a breakdown in mental cohesion and harmony. This phase accumulates a lot of psychic and emotional energy that can be utilized as part of the divergence (for better or for worse). The philosopher Nietzsche, who perhaps recognized this condition better than others, said that under certain circumstances, 'Nihilism might be the sign of a process of incisive and most essential growth, and of mankind's transit into completely new conditions of existence.'[5] This sign of growth is because the human being – the new mutation – is rootless, discontinuous with a past that is being dismantled and destroyed, and is eager for the new apocalypse (i.e., 'revelation') to emerge in its place. And yet, there are simultaneously forces pushing to create the mass-minded collective as opposed to the individualized person. The 'new human' of the devolutionary path will be a reduced version of themselves – the *Robosapien* that is the profane human being. Before human civilization arrives at that juncture (what some have termed as the 'bifurcation'), there is the increasing danger of a rising incoherence that paralyzes people between the extremes of external power and an increasing internal powerlessness. This encroaching 'lucid absurdity' is like the emperor's new clothes where very few people are recognizing the blatant incongruity of our mainstream narratives and so there is almost no one around to ask the question as to how we can transcend the perceptual limits of the world. It would seem that a certain form of inner truth is required for such an enterprise.

Such times of neo-nihilism – a form of ideological and spiritual purposelessness – is when things fall apart because they no longer have any centre to hold them together. And yet a form of daily life continues, similar to Bruegel's depiction of the fall of Icarus[i] which goes unnoticed. The external events of any age are a projection of humanity's inner state and psyche; only that, at certain times this collective condition becomes more visible upon the world stage. During the cycle of transition, or transmutation – of cultural death and rebirth – there are fewer commonly accepted points of orientation, and the compass no longer has a magnetic north. In times of changing magnetics, people are more eager to adopt the obedience to security as an easy external dependency. And yet, nihilism, insecurity, meaninglessness, and lack of purpose, are not the cause but the symptoms. The orientation of the individual is an internal question rather than an external one. The individual has to come to their own sense of coherence. In the words of Václav Havel: 'The principles of control and discipline ought to be abandoned in favor of self-control and self-discipline.'[6] The self/Self has to come to the fore, otherwise an individual is lost to the energetic forces of massification and external manipulation. As we enter these times of the transmutation cycle (octave), we shall be called upon to exhibit our self-control and self-discipline if we are to

---

[i] *Landscape with the Fall of Icarus* currently displayed in the Royal Museums of Fine Arts of Belgium in Brussels.

recalibrate our own state of body, mind, and being. For these are vital times as we make the choice whether we physically and psychically extricate ourselves from the negating forces of chaos and step into a new cycle/octave for humanity.

References

[1] Wilson, Colin (2018/1957) *The Age of Defeat*. London: Aristeia Press

[2] Harari, Yuval Noah (2018) *21 Lessons for 21st Century*. London: Jonathan Cape.

[3] Rose, Seraphim (2018/1994) *Nihilism: The Root of the Revolution of the Modern Age*. Platina, CA: St. Herman of Alaska Brotherhood, p11.

[4] Rose, Seraphim (2018/1994) *Nihilism: The Root of the Revolution of the Modern Age*. Platina, CA: St. Herman of Alaska Brotherhood, p79

[5] Cited in Rose, Seraphim (2018/1994) *Nihilism: The Root of the Revolution of the Modern Age*. Platina, CA: St. Herman of Alaska Brotherhood, p91

[6] Havel, Vaclav (1985) *The Power of the Powerless: Citizens Against the State in Central Eastern Europe*. London: Routledge, p77

Sol

Metaphysics of the Void: deconstructing the nature of the Game within lesser reality

If you are the dealer, let me out of the game
If you are the healer, I'm broken and lame
If thine is the glory, mine must be the shame
You want it darker, we kill the flame

~ Leonard Cohen

There is no 'nothingness' – there is only *everythingness*. There is no void as there is no vacuum, no so-called 'empty space.' There is only energy, frequency, and vibration. Everywhere. The only void that exists is in our beliefs and the illusion that maintains them. The void is our sense of separation from this *everythingness* of energy. And yet we have a constant feeling that we carry around with us, a lingering niggle or a faint residue of memory, that gives us the sense that we are missing something. There is a gap or split in this reality of ours, and yet we rarely perceive this, so enthralled we are with playing our roles – of being within *The Game*. The subjective world is a fiction, and unless we awaken to this 'reality game,' then we are going to give away our roles to others – the controllers, the machines, etc. – and the script will be re-adjusted. This will become the new void where our very consciousness is a dream within the dream of the Machine.

Life within this lesser reality – or 'the Game' – is not dangerous in itself. That is, the open playing field is not dangerous; it is what we put on the field that creates the danger. It is our subjective beliefs, ideals, opinions, and convictions that make it so. Our known reality is a canvas that we paint our visions, our illusions, or our delusions upon. And this reality is an amalgam, an accumulation and fusion, of all our thinking and projected dreams, wishes, ideals, etc. People have martyred themselves for the sake of their beliefs, their sense of truth, their morals or values – yet not for the sake of reality itself. Reality is also like a void. It absorbs everything, sucks everything into itself. It also allows for all possibilities and potentialities. There is no emptiness. That existence is empty is perhaps the grandest illusion. No life is ever empty. The void allows for all and any experience to be gained. Yet there are rules too. Any good game has a minimum of rules, otherwise there would be absolute chaos. Chaos and order abound – but not in absolute terms. The void is both the absorption of all light and also the seeming absence of light: the affirming and the denying. And it reflects, depending upon the capacity of the receiver to perceive (the reconciling). The void is like an ocean: it can seem polluted or crystal clear, depending on whether the mind that perceives is cluttered or cleansed. When the receiver has been cleansed, the reflection of what is beyond appears in it. And here, in this shared reality of humankind, fantasies and delusions occupy people's minds and prevent them from working properly. And then the void appears unstable, unpredictable, and sometimes frightening. Yet it's not the void that frightens people, or a confusion over the nature of reality, or even the sense of meaninglessness. What frightens people is the unknowing, and the sense that perhaps they got it all wrong. And everything they thought, or loved, or put their investment of time and energy into, may not be what they thought it was, or may not be that important or even helpful to them. And then that niggling sense of missing something comes back. And they know that they are out of time, and that they may have to return and repeat the whole game all over again until they start to realize it for what it is.

No one likes to admit that they have been deceived. Worse still, that they got it all wrong and now perhaps they'll need to change how they see things – how they think, believe, and maybe even how they live. No one wishes to learn that they have based their life on a lie, or an illusion. Nietzsche put it well when he said: '… for when you gaze long into the abyss. The abyss gazes also into you.' The void, as I have said, is the *everythingness* upon which reality is constructed. It can neither be created nor destroyed. It is only our belief models of reality that get destroyed or deconstructed and reassembled. The void is the great whole where existence is stripped of its illusions, conditioning, and the added accessories of a physical life. To face the void is to face our inner being and to come to know the self as it has always been. The void upon which existence is etched allows for each incarnated soul to ascribe a new meaning to existence – *their* meaning – instead of accepting the conditioning of the collective mass consciousness. Reality is itself a construction that awaits its own deconstruction. And it can only undergo this dismantling when the perceiver places the inner being as central to their existence. The companion of the void rejects the falsity of the physical world and the false claims made upon reality. Truths can be sought but not gained until first the lies and self-deceptions can be recognized and put aside. Perceptive limitations must first be recognized otherwise one is not able to go beyond them. Gazing into the void (or the 'abyss' as Nietzsche would say) requires complete honesty in the face of life – this is why it deals with the grander questions of existence. We have to strip our prejudices away by first seeing our own prejudices. This is the self-emptying that comes with allowing one to better play the Game. Where did the Game originate? From the Creative Void.

The Game begins with amnesia; a veil of forgetfulness that is wrapped over our senses. And we have until the end of the Game to awaken – to remember. Everything begins with a mystery that very quickly gets turned into normalcy; the everyday; the humdrum tap-tap-tap of our lives. We don't know where we're going and yet we fail to see the beauty of the mystique in this. We fail to be enchanted by the miracle of the everyday because it soon gets locked into a set groove that then becomes the predictable channel of our lives. This consistent groove, like a song track on repeat, keeps people away from prying too far over the top of their reality boxes. There are plenty of false pathways to lead a person down a rabbit hole. The Game is about not being afraid of the answers, whatever they may be, and to never stop questioning. Questions cannot be left aside just to protect illusions or belief sets. The path of the anomaly is a disguise for it leads eventually to lucidity. All mainstream narratives need to be questioned. The strappings of the phenomenal world are like a straitjacket on our senses. And when they are stripped away, what is left? The being of the human remains. It is the being that can exist within the void for it can be nowhere and yet everywhere. The centre can be experienced from the periphery, the circumference. To paraphrase Hermetic wisdom: *Source/Void is a circle whose centre is everywhere and circumference nowhere.*

From the perspective of the void, it is about recognizing that the 'beyond' – the metaphysical – is really at the centre of it all; that the 'beyond' is the very core of existence, and physicality, matter, are trappings added on like decorations. When there is nothing else, all *is*. When there is everything, nothing is. It is the physical existence that becomes the illusion – the front stage in the theatre of life. The world forces us to investigate it through those tools that belong to the world. The lesser reality of the world perpetuates itself by getting everyone to use the same tools created by the illusions of the reality. Everything to a fish will resemble life within the fishbowl. Reality cannot be seen directly for what it is. When we look out at the world, at lesser reality, we are looking into a mirror. Perhaps metaphysics itself is the lie, the delusion, if it is a product of a lesser reality? Yet is metaphysics truly a product of our reality, or does it enter into it from elsewhere, from a realm beyond? After all, meanings are derived from the context of our world, our perceived reality. Perhaps because we have no definitive answers in this world, we create metaphysics to explain a realm beyond our present reality? Humanity exists within a deep ignorance that only deepens the further it dives into materialism, like diving deeper in the depths of the Mariana Trench. Unfathomable mysteries exist only because of our deep ignorance of the world in which we live. Why is there ignorance? Because of the amnesia we carry with us into this incarnation. Why do we arrive with such amnesia? Because that is the nature of the Game. We have to figure out the Game by firstly not knowing about it. We do this by first trying to figure ourselves out. Then we begin to understand what the playing field of the Game is all about and what we can do – or need to do – whilst we are here. Yet this 'awakening,' as it is often termed, is not easy; not easy at all. Why? Because there are too many dreamlike revelries that fill our waking minds. This also is the nature of the Game. Reality, or that which we regard as reality, is a responsive inclusive realm. It is like a living, intelligent gel that conforms to our shapes. Not so much physical shapes but the shape of our thoughts, emotions, our mental projections. Reality is a continual revelation as it reveals itself to us according to *how we are*. It acts like an immune response; it responds to the call of our mind-body. The more we are revealed to ourselves, the more of reality is likewise revealed to us. It is a science. And the only true science is metaphysical. That which is loosely called science, where people prod and poke the matter-energy substrate, is like a child in the sandpit playing with, or throwing around, their toys. Scientists cry too, just as much as the child in its sandpit. Tears of frustration; sometimes of joy and wonder. Yet this science is engaging with a lesser reality, a substratum upon which we stand. We can only make assumptions and speculations about the world. In each step, there needs to be a modicum of observant awareness, for we are not stepping upon known ground but the pebbles of uncertainty. Yet this uncertainty is a necessary ground, for it gives us freedom against the arrogant certainty that weighs us down like granite. The void – the metaphysical centre and circumference – creates revelations through daydreams, and possibilities through the unknown. The void is neither abstract nor non-abstract – it absorbs both and is a merger from which all possibilities can be birthed.

We seek for the 'hidden sense of reality' without realizing that first we need to do the Work. The metaphysics of the void is the metaphysics of the Self. The sun doesn't shine for itself alone. There is no 'metaphysics of the Self' that does not affect others. When we evolve ourselves, we also spread this around us like a ripple effect. And so, by evolving ourselves we can also help to nudge others. There is no separation – no *island of self*. And the metaphysics of the void is the recognition of this unity. There is no separateness of life; this is only a lower order of perception and cognition. The metaphysical view acknowledges the fundamental foundation of unity. Metaphysical seeking is trying to consciously be aware of our merger with Source. A metaphysical understanding is a re-cognition that we are already merged within Source, only that we are operating at a different frequency. The world we know exists as it does for it exists for us as we participate and move through it. Yet it does not exist in the same way for others, for each interprets their steps through the world differently. And some steps are more numb than others. And some steps are comfortably numb. Metaphysics of the void allows for the humanization of reality as well as recognizing it as the lesser reality. It is a case of Hamlet's reply: '*There are more things in heaven and earth, Horatio, than are dreamt of in your philosophy.*' Any distinction must come through intuition and the inner gaze rather than the shortcomings of the outer look. Within the lesser reality, without awareness an individual is an automaton, not dissimilar from a machine; and its consciousness a part of the consensus reality script. Bodies are guided, operating upon minimal cognition.

Mental constructions become a glaze of subjective experience disguised as objective reality. The individual responds to a labyrinth of stimuli as a robotic sensory apparatus. They are receiving yet interpreting little as through a darkened conditioned lens. Perception is as if peering through a slither in the veil.

Human consciousness is largely a reflection of the world, which people often unconsciously receive, gets filtered, and then gets imprinted back onto the lesser reality – and the perception trap sustains itself. Each species has a different type of brain which interprets the world – its environment – differently. The human's perception of the world is not reality itself but rather the brain's representation of reality. Human perception is therefore a roadmap upon the road of lesser reality but is not Reality itself. It can be said to be a simulation of Reality – and humans live within their own specific simulacra. Every degree, or frequency dimension, of reality needs its inhabitants/participants to exist in order to sustain itself. With no one, or no thing, to perceive reality, would it exist for itself alone? Each participant within the shared reality perceives differently. Rotten food for a human may be a gourmet meal for a rat. You may have a rat in your kitchen, yet to the rat it's a whole kingdom. Reality gets reproduced through each individual as a distinct receiver. It is not apprehended *as it is* but through a representation of it. We live within the reflections of reality, gazing indistinctly. People live within their heads more than they realize (and the external power structures – the 'Machine' – know this). Our senses inform us of reality based on specific interpretations of the raw data. Mess with the interpreting process and a different reality ensues. We are as chimeras within a daydream. Our greatest delusion is based on not being able to grasp reality because we are the ones participating in its creation. This is the nature of the lesser reality. And humans go around and around chasing their tails trying to fathom the deep mystery of an 'objective reality' not understanding that they are swimming within their own internal waters. Humans are unable to perceive or comprehend the nature of their existence because they have largely misrepresented their relationship to reality. We are not separate from it any more than our breath is separate from the air. Our deep longing is this inner knowing of how we have created this fundamental separation. We receive signals from the meta-umbilical cord informing us of the separation – and yet, we ignore it believing outer reality to be the Real and our inner knowing to be the ghost. The more we ignore this, the more we become the ghosts. We humanize this separation and make it into the 'suffering of existence' as if this phantasmagorical pain is part of the side-effects of having a physical life.

Our subjective reality is like a fiction – a narrative that is being written – yet we are also the scriptwriters. The script we give ourselves produces the story that we end up living; and this functions both on an individual level as well as collectively. What we view gazing back at us depends upon the nature of our gaze. Humanity creates its own monsters as well as its angels. The story gets entangled through our ongoing fantasies and we expect each person who joins the club to step into the same story. There are even those few groups of 'game bullies' who are trying to push their rules of the Game onto everyone else. They are after a monopoly upon the Game. Human subjectivity being imprinted into the reality pattern can cause feedback loops and constant iterations that eventually produces inherent anomalies. In other words, forms of psychosis arise from these iteration patterns. These viral contagions infest the subjective consciousness field and infect other lesser reality participants. These viral infections are known to be the causes of certain strains of thought that get labelled loosely as 'philosophies.' Nihilism is one such strain; yet it is not a negation of reality but a denial of an objective reality that comes with a set of 'instructions for meaning.' Nihilism can be said to be a recognition, an acknowledgement, of the void from which lesser reality manifests and produces splintered meanings from. It is this perception of the splintering that allows the state of nihilism to exist within the overall Game. Nihilism is not so much a pessimism (although it can exist as such), but rather a confusion over the very fluidity of a subjective lesser reality. Everything can be reconstructed. There is a transparency to our morals and knowledge context – they are only validated by relation to agreement. Nihilism does not need to abide by those agreements, although it can recognize their existence. The 'meaning of life' is therefore neither a problem to be had nor a solution to be defined. It is the *isness* within the flow of all creative potentials within the field of a collectively experienced lesser reality.

Metaphysics of the void can very quickly become over intellectual and mentalized. It then becomes not a practical thing but a thought ogre that wants to be wrestled with. And this can then lead to a form of mental paralysis and/or incubating paranoia. This form of nihilism can sterilize the inner being, whereas a metaphysics of the void is about abundant meaning out of anything, regardless of the physical environment. Metaphysics of the void is a form of *cosmic contentment*, irrespective of physical trappings, programs, and cultural garb. It is the false solidity of the world that refutes the void. Metaphysics recognizes that the physicality of the world is a condition of its particular state but is not its fundamental nature. The essence of life is its fluidity – not its solidity. Within the metaphysics of the void, solidity is a false assumption, a perceptive error. People tend to cling to relative judgements based upon their physical senses. Yet they consider these relative judgements to be more significant than they are. It is easy to form attachments with such judgements and then defend these as if they were fundamental truths. Even if a person has an inward recognition that these judgements may not be secure, they shift to defending their investment in them. However, genuine metaphysics poses no danger to those of sane, balanced mind. People who deny metaphysics, on the other hand, pose a risk to their sanity. Those who live in denial of a metaphysical reality are actually living with a mental disorder. Such people fear emptiness; they may even consider it a threat. They dislike the unknown, and cling to the driftwood of illusory certainty. Without knowing it, such people may subconsciously fear the death of illusion. With unrecognised intention, they rally for the continuation of certainty at all costs – and this is where the Machine has got a power over them.

Nothingness only exists as an idea, a mental concept. For within the unity of Source, nothingness is an impossibility. Nothingness can only exist as a false aspect within the Game – or further, within the phantasmagorical realms of the virtual worlds, for it too is a phantasma. And there is a power-control structure and construct – the 'Machine' – that knowingly manipulates the lesser reality and thus the Game. This power-control structure can be said to have been established and operated by a collective or soul-group; a family of 'hidden hands.' It is the nature of the Machine to distort lesser reality. There are programs of the Machine too that attempt to create negative connotations of the lesser reality experience. We should be aware of the negating programs of the Machine that aim to cultivate fear, anxiety, and anger within the participants of lesser reality. To be alert to those materialistic skeletons that masquerade as silicon prophets. Life can be indistinct, abstract, absurd even. It can seemingly lack meaning, yet this is only a projection from one's own subjective world. If a person encounters meaninglessness, then they have removed themselves from a frequency of unified consciousness and de-synched into a splintered vibration. There is no vacuum in existence – it simply does not nor cannot exist. A vacuum is a myth, a scientific falsity. A barren reality is the projection from a barren mind. It is a mind that vibrates at a machinic frequency. There are those people who seek for a 'barren reality' for they pursue a nihilistic path. It is their program. Many such programs exist (and are supplied) as software for creating a mental terrain decoupled from a harmonic resonance. Such programs may also cultivate the conditioned desire for a state of non-being – that is, a revolt against existence. And some people are just born (incarnated) to be natural saboteurs within the Game. The Machine operates to prevent a true understanding of the nature of Reality. It also seeks to keep people asleep within the Game and unaware of the nature of their cognitive containment field.

Many people live life as if it were a dream. Yet few live it as a lucid dream. We seldom think about managing reality as we've been conditioned to accept that reality manages us. This is a passive perception of reality, not an active one. We literally arrive into physical life with a 'reality screwdriver' in our hands, yet we hardly ever think to use it – or realize it is there. And so, very little seems to get fixed through us. This is the aim of the Machine – to keep us unawares to the rules of the Game. There are also those people who go through life as if they are in mourning or grief. A constant sadness, hopelessness, depression, apathy, and a general lack of interest in the world around them. On the other side of this are those people who seem to live in a constant state of 'emotional emergency,' where every small thing triggers a heightened emotional response. There are too many contaminants within the outer world of lesser reality. They act as contagions, affecting minds, hearts, and bodies. And there is a distinct lack of inner will to counter these intrusions and vital energy infections. The aim of the Machine is to create a spiritual abyss where people seeking their connection to Source will be returned with an empty black hole. But this is because the black hole will be in the exterior, and not the interior. And the fault lies in looking without for what has always existed within, and through the within into the meta/beyond – the Intelligence of All. Life inside the Machine is but a dream. And yet now humanity has arrived at a new stage upon its path, and the threshold ahead beckons. There is no time now to mourn the loss of an old reality for a new perceptive reality awaits. Illusions may move us, but they cannot become an inner driving force. Our illusions within the Game only exist as a provisional stage during this crossing of the threshold. The temporary malaise of the physical world was set up as a trigger to push humankind beyond the threshold. Now, we need to understand the mechanisms of the threshold as it is soon to be upon us.

Fa

The Energetics of Equilibrium, Inertia & Evolvement

As humanity moves through the transition period of the transmutation octave, or cycle, there will inevitably be a split as people align themselves to differing realities and their resonant frequencies. I have mentioned previously in this series of essays how around the period of the juncture, or what some have termed as the 'bifurcation,' there is the increasing danger of a rising incoherence that paralyzes people between the extremes of external power and an increasing internal powerlessness. I also stated that there are always a portion of the populace who are unable to pass the 'threshold of the epoch' in terms of aligning with the frequencies of the incoming developmental impulse. This segment of society may then enter a path of devolvement for the remainder of the epoch as they have left the stream of evolutionary humanity. If developmental impulses are rejected and replaced with degenerative forces or energies, then the path forward for humanity will become severe. If the vital life is replaced by the mechanical, then the qualities/energies of inertia, ignorance, incapacity, and inaction come to the fore. These are the energies that darken, or obscure, the living realm. Such forces dampen the human will and dissolve its degree of concentration. Certain impulses at the current time are aiming to make materialism all-pervading; and we should not be distracted into thinking that the digital realm is not a part of this stream of deep materialism. At the same time, such forces can also work to forward the evolutionary impulses by keeping them from falling into inertia. The push-pull of these seemingly opposing forces can be said to create the bifurcation that gives people a choice over which timeline, or stream, they decide to opt for. Looked at through the physical lens, it would appear that we are standing at the threshold of a global materialistic worldview of life. If the material consciousness remains attached and entangled within the physical, it becomes increasingly difficult for transcendental impulses to penetrate and have effect. Yet if human consciousness can benefit from these constricting and conflicting forces, to move away from physical entanglement and inertia, then

78

a bifurcation is possible that allows for the individual to entrain to the new developmental frequency. This contestation of forces between growth/evolvement and inertia/devolvement is what has been personified in human mythology as the struggle between 'good versus evil.'

What people often call 'evil' is really that which is moving in the contrary direction to the evolutionary stream within the current reality. That is, the word or label 'evil' represents a force that moves toward or aligns with non-existence (another term for evil is disequilibrium). It is a force that holds back or constrains the evolutionary or developmental impulses. That is, it pulls back and restrains this forward movement. If these so-called 'evil forces' are left unopposed, then the momentum towards inertia and stagnation become dominant. However, if the developmental or 'good' forces begin to directly resist the evil forces, then they are consumed by this endeavour and lose, or forfeit, their energies to be used for evolvement. This then also hampers the function of evolvement. These contrary 'evil' or entropic forces of devolvement must instead be dealt with not by direct resistance or attacking them but by either rendering them inert, useless; or by transmuting them into a force that is no longer entropic. As Jesus is recorded as saying: 'But I say, do not resist an evil person! If someone slaps you on the right cheek, offer the other cheek also.' (Matthew 5:39). The restoration of equilibrium that remains dynamic rather than static is part of the function of the interplay between these polarizing forces. Equilibrium – that is, balance and order – keeps the game in play so that it is not pulled toward any one extreme. Yet within this overall fluidity and vitality of seeking equilibrium is the need to allow through enough of the developmental force to maintain a trajectory of evolvement and growth.

In the tradition of the Kabbalah there is the concept of *tikkun*, which refers to the idea that everyone is placed here on Earth to fulfil a particular mission. Another concept of *tikkun* is also that of 'restitution' that, according to Gershom Scholem, refers to the restoration of the ideal order, which forms the original aim of creation, and is also the secret purpose of existence. The restoration of the 'ideal order' – i.e., of equilibrium – is sometimes referred to as 'salvation' in other traditions. Another Kabbalistic concept is that of *kelippot* – defined by Scholem as 'shells,' 'husks, or 'forces of evil' – that seem to also correspond to the notion of the 'hostile forces' in the philosophy of Sri Aurobindo and the Mother. The *kelippot* or shards became the source of gross matter and represent also the source of 'evil.' The *kelippot*, or gross physical matter, have 'sparks of divine light' within them (i.e., the sacred spirit). These sparks of divine light can be redeemed by human actions, and in this way restitution (*tikkun*) will be accomplished and evil will be transformed and overcome. Until this transformation happens, the state of potential disequilibrium (or evil) remains a persistent presence. These vying forces of disequilibrium (entropy, inertia, etc) and evolvement are viewed as representing a grander cosmic process. The question that then arises is: how can human beings hasten the restitution? And this is where various inner developmental or spiritual teachings come into play as an attempt to steer people into, at the least, living a balanced life; and, if/when possible, to participate consciously in the stream of advanced evolvement. Another view on the notion of 'evil' is to see it as a form of ignorance; and as such, they become those forces that work to establish, maintain, and prolong such ignorance among people, communities, and societies. In this view, evil can be said to be like an unconscious abyss; it is a separation from the awareness of Truth. Evil could be said to be those impulses that sustain an individual's perception of separation from Source. And it is this separation from a source, or stream, of vital energies that creates an inertia. And living within this inertia is as living in ignorance and/or falsehood. This ignorance can be maintained by social-cultural agencies wishing to sustain the continuance of this *error*.

Yet life within the density of physical matter inevitably contains this 'error' or falsehood, for this is the nature of the vibratory realm of matter. As such, error – or 'evil' – has its necessary role to play within the whole. In other words, it is a necessary force within the cosmic structure and its processes. The unconscious (the 'abyss') requires to be equilibrated and harmonized with all opposing points of consciousness. Perhaps this 'cosmic play' is about returning to a state of equilibrium. As such, all such forces are indispensable within the life of the cosmos as well as within the Great Work. Transmutation and evolvement are not possible without vying forces of different charge and influence working in dynamic relationship. The same applies to the very constituent parts of materiality: for example, atoms require the positive charge (proton) and negative charges (electron) to be equilibrated in relation to the neutralizing forces (neutrons). In a similar way, the philosopher-mystic George Gurdjieff describes this relationship through the contesting forces of *Holy Affirming* (positive) and *Holy Denying* (negative) leading to a *Holy Reconciling* (neutral/equilibrium). Gurdjieff referred to this as the 'Law of Three.' In this context, we can see how the intermingling of contradictory impulses – such as matter and spirit – is necessary in order to seek resolution that would not only be an integration of these contradictory forces but at the same time a synthesis *greater than* the sum of their parts. This has been referred to in philosophical terms as the dialectical approach whereby an idea (thesis) gives rise to a counter idea (antithesis) and the original idea and counter idea merge to give rise to a new idea (synthesis). Or, using Gurdjieff's terminology, the Holy-Affirming force (active) attracts a Holy-Denying force (reactive), and this contestation leads to a resolution of the Holy-Reconciling (unifying). Similarly, Rudolf Steiner noted how the fusion of these opposing principles is necessary for giving the human being a self-conscious force for evolvement: 'It is this fusion of opposing principles which makes evil possible for man, but it also gives him the power of self-consciousness, choice and freedom . . .'[1]

From this author's perspective, negating forces can seemingly interfere with an individual's mental field, or field of consciousness, infiltrating it with heavy and dark thoughts, leading to a psychological imbalance if they are not neutralized through counteractive impulses. That is why the path of inner work requires that a person maintain a state of balance – mentally, emotionally, and physically – at all times. Yet such interferences may still be necessary at particular stages of the transformational work. What we consider to be the 'worst adversaries' or negative influences are still a part of the overall cosmic manifestation that can, consciously or not, assist others in the great work of developmental transformation. It can be said that all earthly things are born in darkness and must themselves seek the light. Just as the plant is first seeded in the dark soil, it seeks the light for its own inner transformative processes through photosynthesis. So too do humans need to cultivate their own form of photosynthesis – i.e., of synthesizing the light – for their developmental growth. Too much focus and emphasis upon the material (the dark earth) will create an unbalanced materialistic tendency. The extreme of this will lead to a splintering, or separation, away from metaphysical impulses. The physicalizing of metaphysical impulses is one of the falsehoods and deceptions of the negating forces. The soft-science of the quantum spiritualists is a case in point here. The notion of quantum entanglement can snare a person within the physical manifestation resulting from entanglement if they have not done sufficient work upon their own inner state. It is yet another false pathway of distraction whereby tempting shortcuts are dressed up in delightful 'spiritual science' that take people's focus away from the inner path. And on the other side, too much immersion into the 'spiritual path' can take a person into a 'la-la-land' of crystal gazing and detach them from the responsibilities and necessities of participating within a physical life experience. At the current time of writing, it does seem that the negating forces of disequilibrium and inertia are taking dominance in what could result in the temporary rise of tyranny within our physical institutions and systems.

The Inertia of Tyranny

The power structures that come to constitute a social totalitarian order attempt to create a cultural narrative with the aim of presenting their system to be in agreement with a natural human order as well as a universal order. This is the illusion of 'normalcy' within tyranny which it seeks to establish. In other words, the forces of chaos or enforced rule present themselves as a form of natural order. This is chaos and inertia masquerading as order and development. The external world of physical existence attempts to impose itself over the metaphysical order of *beingness*. And yet, as Vaclav Havel presciently noted:

> The whole power structure could not exist at all if there were not a certain metaphysical order binding all its components together, interconnecting them … This metaphysical order is fundamental to, and standard throughout, the entire power structure; it integrates its communication system and makes

possible the internal exchange and transfer of information and instructions … This metaphysical order guarantees the inner coherence of the totalitarian power structure. It is the glue holding it together, its binding principle, the instrument of its discipline.[2]

The world of appearances is not without its unseen forces offering their energies of contestation, whether these be classed as 'metaphysical' or not. The danger here is that as an outward 'world of appearances' gains in dominance and extremity, it loses connection with the balancing forces and begins to mutate into a ritualistic realm of signs and totems and migrates increasingly into a pseudo-state of artificial construct that becomes the consensus reality. And as this newly mutated consensus reality, it gains strength as a form of tyranny or totalitarian power. It may even get to the stage where it has replaced any prior connection with reality – or the 'Real' – and becomes a self-contained reality itself, albeit one formed through artificial forms of power and control. The ritual has overtaken the presence of the reality hidden behind it. Or, put another way, 'the significance of phenomena no longer derives from the phenomena themselves.'[3] And this is why a physical system of tyranny and power has an inertia built into it, as it focuses and directs its energy on defending the false integrity of the world of appearances in order to sustain itself. Such a system attempts to seal itself off hermetically from developmental impulses in a bid to retain the status quo. They may even develop technologies that appear progressive; yet these are all cut-off from the vital forces of life and thus an inertia will creep into the entire system that will eventually bring it into disorder and either stagnation and/or breakdown.

Any social system that does not tap into the impulses of evolvement, and the vital metaphysical forces, will have no real lasting power as it relies on a form of automation and mechanical motive power. The energetics of control and discipline are not as dynamic as those corresponding yet contrary energies of self-control and self-discipline. The force required to maintain the structures of an automated and mechanized system, lacking any connection to developmental impulses, is great indeed and cannot be maintained in the long term. The forces of inertia will creep into any socio-cultural system that relies on automatism, including that of a global technological civilization. The potential failure of modern humanity will come from choosing to step away from the vibrational threshold of heightened consciousness in favour of a future predicated upon the restriction of human cognitive capacities and a disconnect from metaphysical influences and the life of vital spirit.

References

[1] Steiner, *An Esoteric Cosmology: Eighteen Lectures Delivered in Paris, France, May 25 to June 14, 1906.* (Rudolf Steiner Archive.)

[2] Havel, Vaclav (1985) *The Power of the Powerless: Citizens Against the State in Central Eastern Europe.* London: Routledge, p10

[3] Havel, Vaclav (1985) *The Power of the Powerless: Citizens Against the State in Central Eastern Europe.* London: Routledge, p11

Shock Two

Is There Life on Earth?
(A Thought Experiment)

Sometimes to advance along a train of thought it is necessary to be shaken away from the main highway and to take a different track – to receive a 'shock' (such as in a thought experiment). This is one of those, as it helps to provide an energetic impetus for the final part of the transmutation octave. Let us speculate upon the seeds of life, and what may be the reasons, or function, for human life to exist on this planet. We shall begin by taking a Gurdjieffian approach on the matter.[ii]

All life in the universe, it is said, exists at differing rates of vibration. And these differing rates correspond to their state of emanation, or manifestation. In this, there is

---

[ii] For those readers unfamiliar with the name of G.I. Gurdjieff, it may be beneficial to look him up.

a chain, ray, or hierarchy in states of vibration. That is, there are gradations of existence, with all higher emanations integrated or forming a part of all lower gradations; but, of course, the lower gradations do not form part of the higher emanations. These vibrational energies, then, flow (to use a vague and imprecise term) from less dense into denser conditions (again, a vague analogy). Yet this movement, or trajectory, of vibrations is not linear and inevitable. In other words, if left alone, such a movement runs into difficulties. At various stages of this vibrational flow, assistance is required. And this is where the thought experiment now turns to life on this planet, the Earth (as we named it). The frequency emanations within this universe flow from the Absolute to all other grand arrangements or systems of Intelligence (galaxies, nebulae, etc.) They then vibrate down to specific galaxies (such as 'our' Milky Way); and next onto stars, such as 'our' sun. After the star, the vibrations emanate into the further density of planets (the planets of 'our' solar system), before reaching specific planets that, for us, signifies the Earth. Finally, after the level of a singular planet, the final vibrations reach the densest state where we would find those 'dead' or undeveloped planetoids or satellites, such as what we would call the Earth's moon. So far, so good. But not so good, as the vibrations between the level of the planetary system and the specific planet (Earth) have a problem. Rather, it can be said that there is a situation (for every problem is likewise a situation, but not every situation is necessarily a problem). And what is this 'situation'? Well, it's like this. The vibrations are having a difficult time 'stepping down' from the planetary system level to the level of the Earth. It is similar to how electricity is usually transmitted across the planet: often, heavy voltages of electricity need to be stepped down, or passed through a transformer (a step-down transformer), in order for it to be received at the other end. If the electricity leaving the power station did not pass through a step-down transformer before reaching our homes, every fuse and device in our homes would be blown, and the house circuit would be fried. The same applies to the Earth – it needs some form of a step-down transformer. Welcome to the entry of organic life.

When I say organic life, I am referring in this thought experiment not to all organic life but specifically to that species which got nominated to represent the 'step-down transformer' role. And yes, you guessed correctly – this happens to be the human species. The human being, consciously or unconsciously – and the point here is that it's mostly unconscious – functions as a transmitter of vibrations that are necessary for the evolution of the planet Earth. Humanity acts as a form of membrane across the surface of the planet and is receptive to the myriad of vibrations, emanations, and all other types of influence that are arriving to the planet from the solar environment. No wonder then that human beings act so erratically if they are the buffer (after the Earth's magnetic shielding) to receive whatever is coming in. And, we must assume, there is a lot coming in. And at times when the Earth's magnetic shielding is particularly diminished, such as now, there is a greater exposure to the full force of the incoming vibrations. If we are to take this thought experiment one step further, and staying with the Gurdjieffian perspective, it can be said that humans not only transmit the incoming stepped-down energies but that they also produce energies of their own. After all, through our physical labours we are generating energy, are we not? Where does this energy go to? It may be that our energies are being passed along to the next level to contribute to the chain of developmental transmission. And next in line is the Earth's satellite – the moon. And so, in this context it can be said that humans, during their physical existence, are generating energies to *feed the moon*. And yet, almost all the step-down transformer and moon-feeding energies are generated unconsciously. Human beings are being utilized as energy transformers and generators. And what do we get out of it? Well, we get to have the experience of a physical lifetime. Fair trade off? The question that may next get asked is: why do we need to participate in this unconsciously? Because, it could be surmised, that humans would not be willing otherwise to give away these energies. If everyone suddenly awakened to the fact that we were giving away so much potential energies, don't you think we may wish to renegotiate this position in order to preserve some energies for ourselves? And here comes the crux.

Humanity can develop and evolve as a mass, yet this is slow going. This rhythm, however, is the 'mass speed' and moves together as a collective. Yet, like any well-organized collective, there are always scouts that are sent on ahead to be pioneers and prepare the way. If you wanted to use a fancy word, you could call these the 'evolutionary outriders.' A vibrational pattern needs to be set-up, just like establishing a blueprint as a foundation for what is to come. These 'outriders' go on ahead and work to utilize available energies (those incoming and those from self) to establish a vibrational resonance for the next phase of the developmental impulse. In order for this to occur, a few people need to 'make themselves available,' as it were, for the accumulation of energies for this use. And this means that they are not disposed for giving their energies for the feeding of the moon. Some may say that this is not a just or fair situation as why should a small minority of individuals get to use their energies for means other than being a step-transformer buffer for the Earth and as food for the moon? Well, quite simply put, not that many people are actually striving to be *conscious* individuals. The opportunity is there for all, so to speak – yet few are those who respond. So, the only barrier to inclusion is the individual themselves. And this, it can be suspected, has always been the case. The question now to be asked in this thought experiment is: is this good enough?

Life upon planet Earth is an experiment, let us say, and the human species is being monitored to see how it performs in its allotted role as transformers and transmitters of vibrations. What if, now that a sufficiently prolonged period of time has elapsed, it has come to the attention of the advanced Intelligence monitoring the progress upon this planet that humans are, well, falling down on the job. What if humans are no longer functioning well in this role and so a new 'transmitter model' is required? Time is up for humanity. What form could possibly replace humanity to act as this buffer zone between the solar neighbourhood and the Earth? Welcome to the rise of the machines.

The Machinic Transformer

No great surprise here as the planet Earth is already being terraformed to accommodate the rising technological ecosystem. Any sufficiently advanced species visiting this planet could be forgiven for thinking that a terraforming project is underway for adapting the planet Earth for a machinic intelligence or A.I. form of species. The highly dense electromagnetic environment, the masts and antennas, the cameras and surveillance systems, the WIFI relay stations, the profusion of low earth orbit satellites, etc., and more, are establishing a network – a digital architecture – that could act like an A.I. semi-sentient global brain capable of receiving the cosmic vibrations, step-transforming and re-transmitting them, effectively putting humanity out of a job (a purpose). Wouldn't that be a haunting thought?

Perhaps this is why there has arisen the drive towards a transhumanist future where a machinic intelligence overtakes the two-legged, three-brained, carbon-bodied human species as the dominant player for the next phase of Earth's evolution. Yet this, however, could also indicate a new impulse to develop a sense of purpose for human life in relation to the rise of an A.I. architecture of intelligence. In order to retain their 'usefulness' a certain percentage of humanity will be compelled to develop their innate psychic abilities – to activate their latent organs of perception. Those persons incapable of turning inward will probably choose to 'merge' with the machinic intelligence so as to perpetuate some semblance of their

DNA as a recombinant element with code: silicon-carbon recombinant life force. This new cyborgian species would then become the 'new model' replacement to take on the function of being an energy transformer and transmitter. Still, it seems that the transhumanist route will not be for the majority as it is largely being peddled by an elite class of techno-nerds and bonkers billionaires. The machinic A.I. substitution could benefit humanity in another way, for whilst the Earth needs a 'transmitter' membrane to fulfil its function, this requirement means that the majority of humanity needs to remain relatively unconscious to their purpose. That is, they are occupied with everything other than their inner developmental potential. But once there is an A.I. substitution for the job, the human worker gets relieved of duty, so to speak. By having a replacement or 'surrogate species' in this role, then humanity would be freed from this role necessity and can shift into a new stage of evolvement. The human species would be given a free run to 'work' upon itself to evolve and 'create a soul' (as they say) in order to participate in the cosmic evolutionary scheme and to be of use at a higher level in the creative hierarchy. As suggested, this could likely mean a path of development upon the psychic level as part of utilizing the faculties of an extended mind. Whilst A.I. and machinic intelligence take on greater roles in managing and arranging affairs upon the physical plane, human beings will be reaching out to the stars with their minds – cosmic communication with conscious intention. However, if humanity collectively fell back into a state of unconsciousness, then the advanced Intelligence monitoring the progress upon this planet may decide that the experiment has failed and that the human species has entered a dead-end evolutionary pathway and, as such, are no longer required. The human experiment would be allowed to eventually die off. After all, there is now an A.I. substitute to keep the transformer-transmitter role operational for the planet Earth and its satellite moon. But wait there. That all sounds a bit drastic, doesn't it? I'm sure that humanity, being the immature and largely infantile species that they are, would at least be given a final chance, or even a push, to 'up its game' before the machines take over? Ah, now that brings us to the present time and the post-pandemic human condition.

The Pandemic Shockwave

As part of this continuing thought experiment, we can perhaps entertain the consideration that the global pandemic of 2020-21 was a last 'shock' to give humanity a final chance to push past a necessary threshold upon its developmental trajectory. Of course, this is just pure speculation here – a kind of mental play for the mind. Continuing with our Gurdjieffian approach on the matter, just as the octave of cosmic vibrations requires a shock-style interval to get it past a certain part of its journey, so too does humanity have a proclivity within itself whereby, at certain intervals, it becomes 'stuck,' so to speak. And when at this juncture of 'stuckness' or blockage, humanity requires some outside intervention to jolt it sufficiently to get it past a teetering threshold. As human civilization on this planet, at this current time, is straggling through a period of deep materialism, cultural vulgarity, and widespread psychological malaise, it seems an ideal time to receive an unexpected jolt to kickstart a new phase of developmental activity. It's just a thought here (as this is only a thought experiment), yet wouldn't it be convenient that as the recent global pandemic began to usher in a recalibrated multi-polar world order, it might also have stimulated a new phase of human evolvement within a conscious segment of the human species. This may not be the case; yet then again, it also could be the case. Every non-possibility also includes its inherent contrary possibility. The question, as always, is whether anything will result from these potentials.

The human species is forever in potential, and never in completion. Modern human civilization has made great advancements upon the physical world stage. In terms of technology and material gains there has been incredible progress. Yet psychologically and in a spiritual sense, it can be said that humanity is losing pace. And this can lead to a serious predicament where the technological possibilities within our grasp are not fully aligned with a level of conscious awareness and perceptive ability to fully understand the situation before us. We are overwhelmed with information, yet we lack the comprehension and knowledge to gain an understanding of how to manage our predicament. Things could get out of hand very quickly and very easily. In such circumstances it may be said that a *jolt* is very badly needed.

Returning to the title of this thought experiment – *Is There Life on Earth?* – we may still be able to answer in the affirmative; but does this include the future state of the human being? And will it include human sentient life in the majority – or will a machinic intelligence be the majority case and a conscious humanity a lesser percentage? In other words, if the 'pandemic shock' was applied to be just that – a jolt for human inner development – then will the call be heeded? Perhaps it does not need to be heeded by the majority; it may all correspond to who has ears to hear and eyes to see.

And in this manner, we may now close down this thought experiment as no doubt only a few ears, and even fewer eyes, were on the page – or on the ball. An interesting and partly entertaining distraction perhaps. Onwards to the main octave and back into the fray of the great heresy.

Mi

The Grand Heresy

Metaphysics is not so much about that which is 'beyond' physics as this suggests that what is metaphysical lies only in the beyond zone and not within. The metaphysical fire, which has correspondence to Origin, Source, and Intelligence of All, is behind time, space, causation and manifestation, as well as being integrated as all those aspects. The metaphysical fire is as much *beyond* as it is *within*, for there is never a state that is void of it – even the void itself is an expression of the metaphysical fire. In Cabbalistic terms, there are four levels of reality, or emanations: Divine, Spiritual, Psychological, and Physical. The Divine corresponds to the Source of All (SoA); the Spiritual is Non-Being, or what modern science refers to as the quantum vacuum, zero-point field, the implicate order, or the void. The Psychological is the first manifestation or Being; again, what science would call the cosmic background radiation or cosmic energy. And the Physical is the world of matter, organisms, and of material sense. These are gradations of existence, with all higher emanations integrated or forming a part of all lower gradations. In other words, the physical realm of matter contains the psychological, the spiritual, and the Divine – only that they are hidden to plain view (perception). What this means is that the metaphysical impulse (or Fire/Light) is existent – *hidden within* – all states of existence, including our material realm. And this, for much of human history, has been a grand heresy.

It is not necessary here to go through a historical stocktake of heresies (the list would be very long!), yet even a passing glance would pick up Gnostic trails (including Catharism, Manichaeism), mystical and occult streams, and almost anything that tackles the dogmatic control structures of orthodoxy. Heresy has been an easy and cheap strategy to attack and dismantle perceived threats against dominant narratives. Heresy has been the label that stigmatizes those people, thinking, beliefs, ideologies, and movements, etc, that defy or go against the ruling narratives and control apparatus of the time. Heresies also help to point out to those with critical awareness that they live under a form of totalitarianism, in some degree or other. Such socio-cultural control apparatuses seek to indoctrinate the populace within their domain into accepting specific thinking patterns. These patterns, naturally, are established to reinforce and support the incumbent power systems. The concept of heresy is brought out and utilized as a means of involving people – the 'public' – within the controlling system. In an age of secularization, the controlling narrative has shifted from a top-down religious power structure into a technologically enforced 'cage of modernity.' This is akin to sociologist Max Weber's notion of the 'Iron Cage;' or more recently, to writer Philip K. Dick's vision of the 'Black Iron Prison.' The new secular materialism is bringing forth technocratic governance as a dominating narrative, and its affiliated religion of transhumanism is providing for the next priestly class of tech-elites and billionaires. Together they establish what will strive to become the governing apparatus of technocracy – the modern totalitarian system masquerading as the new mode of 21st century global authority. And the notion of heresy has been modified from quasi-religious sectarian cults into conspiracy. The modern-day heretic is now the much-derided conspiracy theorist, or anyone who dares to defy the consensus narratives. From time immemorial the dominant control apparatus has sought to centralize its power, and this means it must denounce any recognition of direct access to knowledge, which it views as an opposing power and thus a direct threat. Also, the external apparatus of the hierarchical control system cannot be reflected in a metaphysical hierarchical system. For this reason, the Christian Church did not wish for a 'hierarchy of angels' to become recognized, although we have such people as Pseudo-Dionysius the Areopagite and Thomas Aquinas to thank for bringing these systems into human cognition and awareness. Material power structures do not care for metaphysical realities to come out of hiding. This is why such perspectives are branded as heretical and their proponents persecuted into silence or death.

A metaphysical perspective is one that recognizes how all existence is integrated and unified, and that what lies without also lies within for there is no exterior, only internal degrees or gradations of perceptual experience (existence). The phenomenal universe of which we observe and participate within is a lesser reality – a reflection or gradation from the unifying Greater Reality. It is within this lesser reality that our current 'Game of Life' is playing out. A modern heresy is that of the simulation hypothesis which states that human existence is not in fact 'real' but being played out within a simulated structure or game. This is an update of the ancient Gnostic perspective that humanity is living within a reality created not by Source but by a Demiurge (a 'lesser god'), and in this sense it is somewhat a false reality. Whether we are avatars or amnesiac souls within material bodies, the playground is relatively the same. What the simulation hypothesis does is merely update the scenario based on modern vocabulary and context. The Gnostics didn't have computers in their day (and hence the computer vocabulary); likewise, the modern tech-gnostics (or neo-gnostics) don't wish to speculate within the context of Christian or any other religious-spiritual theology. The overarching situation is one whereby seekers of each age are attempting to penetrate into the nature of the human condition vis-à-vis its correspondence with the true nature of Reality. Modern terminology is now required to pinpoint the attention and focus of the modern-orientated individual. You don't need to be religious in order to accept the Greater Reality. The Absolute is not a bearded bloke or a jealous deity of judgement. Belief is not necessary when it comes to approaching Reality for belief is merely an early stage upon the path of realization. You only need an urge to wonder; an inner pull to know; and the will to seek. The metaphysical fire wishes to be known – and you only need to want to know it too. If we can speak of anything, we can call it a law of resonance. The Knower and the Known must frequent the same frequency for there to be a correspondence. This is the 'field' where the meeting has to take place – a 'field' of frequency as well as a zone of correspondence. As the Persian mystic-poet Jalāl al-Dīn Rumi wrote:

> *"Out beyond ideas of wrongdoing and rightdoing,*
> *there is a field. I'll meet you there.*
> *When the soul lies down in that grass,*
> *the world is too full to talk about.*
> *Ideas, language, even the phrase "each other"*
> *doesn't make any sense.*
> *The breeze at dawn has secrets to tell you.*
> *Don't go back to sleep.*
> *You must ask for what you really want.*
> *Don't go back to sleep.*
> *People are going back and forth across the doorsill*
> *where the two worlds touch.*
> *The door is round and open.*
> *Don't go back to sleep."*

This field exists beyond our localized ideas and morality codes. The physical, sensory world is too full of the lower vibrations – 'too full to talk about' – and this can block the perceptive senses. The ideas and language of the material realm have no meaning within the 'frequency field' that provides 'the doorsill where the two worlds touch.' Yet the seeker must resist being pulled back into the denser senses and lower frequency of the physical realm – 'Don't go back to sleep.' Rumi, and many others like him, clothed themselves within the robes of their time, be it Islam or any other socio-cultural-religious context that was necessary to operate within. The metaphysical impulse knows how to roam unimpeded within the contexts and circumstances of the time. Its core frequency is not of this realm, yet it acts through operations – 'manifestations' – that are of the physical domain. Religious and spiritual vehicles have been utilized as carriers for these manifestations, yet they are certainly not the only means. It also depends upon what the main mediums are at the time within any specific culture. These are often appropriated for maximum dispersal; yet many more mediums, largely unsuspected, are simultaneously utilized for this purpose. The 'heretics' are the visible ones; the grand heresy remains hidden within and operates largely without hindrance. And the Grand Heresy of the *metaphysical fire* still rages in our times. Unfortunately, most people remain oblivious to this. They have fallen asleep amongst the meadows of attractive flowers and amid the scents that tempt the senses. However, an odd and troublesome wind is now blowing through those meadows and disturbing peoples' sleep.

The flowery meadows are not so cosy anymore as an ill wind is stirring those who slumber and arousing people through discomfort and disarray. Uncertainty looms everywhere; the façades of normalcy are slipping down, and the trusted institutions of this reality are showing their false faces. The metaphysical fire is beginning to burn away the outer paintwork, showing the rotten wood underneath. The gatekeepers of stolen power are attempting to cover up the sun by spraying their chemical clouds; yet still, the metaphysical fire comes through. And it is becoming fiery now. It is coming close to another round of its cycle. Flares, outbursts, and eruptions will soon be blasting towards our physical sphere as we cling to its surface like a receiving-transmitting membrane. And it shall all be a matter of frequency. As the great inventor and receiver Nikola Tesla said: *If you want to find the secrets of the universe, think in terms of energy, frequency and vibration.* Any vibrational frequency can create as well as destroy, depending upon the corresponding frequency of the receiver. The Grand Heresy is arising to meet the Dogmatic Destroyer. As the metaphysical fire comes to light, and to alight, our domain, we shall have the fire to guide us or to burn us. No hazmat suits will protect the unprepared. It shall all be a question of perception. Is the heresy a greater truth? Or do the dominant consensus narratives speak the truth to us? As Above, So Below – all is in correspondence. Hiding within the shadowy rock of Plato's cave will not shield you from the penetrating fire. It is only the

108

metaphysical fire that does not burn. Instead, it fills the cells of the body with a heightened, finer energy and renews the human vessel. The time is approaching where we shall need to march forward and go forth upon a new path. We can choose to stay within the rocky, shadowy cave; or we can walk lighter upon the sunlit path.

No amount of machinery will lighten the human vessel – it will only serve to automate it further and close down its receptors. Like any fuel cell, it will eventually wind down to a stop if it cannot be recharged. The devolutionary path is strewn full of those objects that came to their final stop when the fuel cell ran dry. It was, and remains, a closed pathway. You only get so far, despite the shiny promises offered at the beginning. You can take the high road, or you can take the low road. According to Celtic legend, if someone dies in a 'foreign land,' their spirit will travel back to their homeland by 'the low road,' which is known as the route for the souls of the dead. However, the person who takes the 'high road' may arrive afterwards, yet they retain their life. This legend implies that those who accept the high road will continue upon the path of the living, whilst those who take the low road will take their leave of this world and no doubt be obliged to return again – like a Groundhog Day for the soul.

In these coming years, the metaphysical fire shall be burning stronger against the structures of our physical world. Taking refuge in ignorance, rage, or revenge, will not align the individual's receptors towards recalibration. Trust in the human spirit will be a first step; aligning with the resonance of the human heart shall be the second. Being receptive and allowing a new frequency of spirit to come through may be the third. In all this, the greatest barrier and impediment is fear. As circumstances become increasingly polarized, the choices of fear or revelation shall become ever more visible. The dark cave is the refuge of the fearful. The sunlit path is the abode for the revellers of the revealed.

Re

The Demiurge Perspective
&
The Artificial God

*'... it can be said in all truth that "the end of a world"
never is and never can be
anything but the end of an illusion.'*

~ Rene Guenon

Transmutation and transfiguration can still occur within a realm of illusion. Illusion does not necessarily mean that something is intrinsically wrong but rather that something results from a misinterpreted perception. And this is why humanity exists within a realm of illusion because it so far lacks the requisite tools – that is, cognitive capacities – to perceive correctly in alignment with Truth. As the writer Idries Shah put it:

'Yes, the world is an illusion. But Truth is always being shown there.'[1] At each stage of the transmutation octave/cycle of humanity, we are collectively gaining new organs of perception that allow us to grasp deeper and more subtle layers of our reality. Until the present time, our ideas and notions about 'life, the universe, and everything' have been quite limited (despite our vanity in human progress and advancement). This misinterpreted perception, or perceptive limitation, applies to all our areas of understanding, whether it be religious/spiritual, scientific, and everything in-between.

When religious utterance refers to the 'Creator,' or creative intelligence, behind our universe it tends to frame this Creator figure as *the* god. This also may be a product of the human illusion (perceptive lack), for we are yet to grasp the underlying purpose and meaning behind this universe; or what we refer to casually as *our* universe. Many teachings and traditions have attempted to point out this misinterpretation by stating that this universal creation is not so much the creation of the Absolute 'One God' but rather is the creation of a Universal Intelligence – a Demiurgic Intelligence. And that this universe in which we exist is part of a much grander scheme of creation within a far vaster 'cosmic drama' that contains many acts or processes of descent (emanation) and return. There are emanations from the original Source or

112

Absolute. These emanations, planes, or vibratory frequencies (dimensions) have their intermediaries seemingly within a form of hierarchy. These intermediaries operate within a constructive or evolutionary nature. There are also negating or negative entities that form a struggle – or polarity – with the affirming forces and this struggle forms the basis of a movement back to the original state of Source/Absolute. And this is the notion of restitution (which has been translated into the term 'salvation').

Through this understanding it can be stated that the Demiurge is the 'Great Entity' for our universe. It is the creator and sustainer of the universe and its evolution. It is 'our God' but is not the central stillness, the Absolute Unmanifest. The Demiurge manifests from the Absolute Unmanifest and 'takes its place' within a particular zone or point within the manifest Cosmos. From here, it takes on the organization of what we would call 'our universe,' which is under the influences of the greater Cosmos, and this includes also its negative or destructive phases. The Demiurge strives to establish its Universe through the balancing and harmonizing of all its internal elements, which are interior to itself and therefore within its own awareness, or consciousness. The Universe is this one whole Being, and a change or shift in one part affects and/or is registered by all other parts within the Being.

Once internal balance is obtained within the Universe Being, evolution then passes onto the next phase, and so on, until it reaches the organisms within the Universe. Our universe, and all that exists in it, is within the awareness (the 'Mind') of this Great Entity or Demiurge. For all those entities within the Universe, the Demiurge is infinite and omnipotent (i.e., its 'god'). Yet each Universal Demiurge is conditioned by – that is, in correspondence to – the Greater Cosmos of which it is a part.

In certain terminology, the Demiurge is also called the Logos. It is an aspect of the greater Cosmic Consciousness; it is self-aware and then seeks objective consciousness through its own projected mind as its universe. There is a reciprocity between the Demiurge-Logos and its projected universe, as there would be between subject-object. In this case, the Demiurge-Logos is the subject and the universe the object. The Demiurge's focus is upon the universe, and in this it can be said to be 'limited' for it remains within this domain of awareness. Yet another aspect of the Demiurgic consciousness – what we may refer to as its 'subconsciousness' – is aware of the greater Cosmic Consciousness. The movements within Cosmic Consciousness, such as the 'ebb and flow' of its planes of movement, exert forces and influences upon the Demiurgic consciousness, which then get projected, or expressed, through conscious awareness within the universe (for the universe is a projection of its own mind). Reactions and/or modifications to these cosmic influences can then be taken within the universe of the Demiurge. It is similar to a person making a conscious decision to take action, or modify thought, based on a 'nudge' or 'inclination' felt from their subconscious. The subconsciousness of a person passes on an 'influence' that once cognized – or recognized consciously – a person may decide to act upon. And so, it is the same within the mind/universe of the Demiurge: when it receives such influences within its awareness from the greater Cosmic Consciousness of which it is a part it may 'act' upon these, such as by applying modifications to its universe. The universe – what people generally refer to as *our universe* – exists as the mind of the Demiurge that is itself a constituent part of a Greater Cosmos. What human religions (and therefore most people) refer to as 'God' is a Great Entity that is the 'creator' of our particular universe; yet this Logos/Demiurge is itself only one 'Entity' within a far vaster Cosmos that itself is manifested from the Absolute Unmanifest (the Central Stillness).

The consciousness of an individual is usually unable to conceive of its 'god' – or rather, the consciousness of the Demiurge – let alone perceive it, for the individual exists under too many 'laws.' That is, the consciousness of an individual exists under too many iterations away from the primal, basic or original perception. It could be said that human consciousness is under too many layers, as in the Matryoshka Russian dolls, where the original essence (tiniest doll) is overlayered by many larger dolls. The final iteration (the largest of the dolls) is too far removed from its original essence (the smallest doll) to be able to have perceptive clarity, or cognition, of the Demiurgic mind. Another way to put this is that as humanity moves further away from contact with the Great Entity, the Demiurge-Logos, it 'solidifies' (takes on more layering) and becomes further embedded into materialism. It then substitutes the loss of its innate, natural powers and capabilities by seeking mastery over the technological realm. Yet immersion into technology (and thus the digital worlds) is yet a further iteration away from contact with the Demiurgic mind. This comprehension of the cosmic hierarchy now puts forward greater levels of nuance, so that our original 'god-mind' is an intermediary between us and the Absolute.

Similarly, in the cosmic philosophy of the Indian sage Sri Aurobindo, there is the Overmind (the Demiurge), and the greater Supermind (the Absolute Unmanifest). Most mystical and/or esoteric teachings recognize an Absolute that is comprehended through its multiple aspects, or emanations/manifestations. In various teachings the

Absolute has been referred to as *Brahman* (Hinduism/Vedanta); the *One* (Platonism); *Jehovah/God/Allah* (Judaism/Christianity/Islam); the *Pleroma* (Gnosticism); and there are other variations. What they all point to is that there is a 'hierarchy of worlds' that manifest through various planes of existence. These manifestations – or emanations – are knowable or accessible according to perceptive capacities. These emanations are both involutionary (going further away from the Absolute) as well as evolutionary (moving toward the Absolute). In some systems it is said that the involutionary forces move from a higher conscious to a lesser conscious state; and the evolutionary forces are moving from a lesser to a greater conscious state, and they often intermingle during these involutions and evolutions (depicted in Hinduism as the exhale-inhale breaths of Brahman). It is when the involutionary forces are approaching a high degree of their lesser conscious state that they are sometimes regarded as being opposing/negating/hostile forces for the evolutionary impulse moving toward greater consciousness.

Going back to Sri Aurobindo's cosmic philosophy, we see that the Overmind, as the Demiurge-Logos of the universe (the 'Great Entity'), is an emanation itself from the Supermind (Absolute), and this is where we also encounter the levels of imperfection – for any state lesser to the Absolute is, by degrees, less than the perfection of the Absolute. As previously mentioned, the Demiurge is the effective creator of the physical universe (our known universe), and this corresponds also with many Gnostic teachings. In the dualistic forms of Gnosticism, which consider the physical universe to be fundamentally imperfect, the Demiurge-Logos is regarded as a flawed or even as an evil entity/Intelligence. It is worth mentioning here the Gnostic text translated as 'The Reality of the Rulers' (also sometimes translated as the *Nature of the Rulers* or the *Hypostasis of the Archon*) that is believed to have been originally composed in Greek sometime in the second or third century AD/CE.[2] This text puts forth a Gnostic creation myth that states that the creation of the material world (the universe) was done through an evil or 'fallen' Demiurgic Intelligence. Further, there are minions that function in service to the Demiurge (the 'rulers' in the title) that are also referred to as 'archons,' and it is these lesser intelligences (sometimes also referred to as 'demonic beings') which attempt to keep rule by imprisoning the 'souls of humankind' in the material world.

However, to frame an emanation of the Absolute as 'less than perfect' is one thing, but to automatically consider this lesser state to be evil is perhaps a flawed statement in its own right. What this framing does consider is that whilst the Demiurge of this universe may seem godlike to us human mortals, the universe is itself evolving within the grander, macro-Cosmos. As such, the universe we call 'ours' is less than perfect and is itself part of a much larger evolutionary process. And all life existent in this universe is a part of this overarching evolving mind, for it is an emanation from the Demiurgic Intelligence. Regarding the character of the Overmind, Sri Aurobindo wrote in the autumn of 1950, only a few months before his death, that it was 'a subordinate power of the Supermind: it is still an agent of the Truth-consciousness, a gnostic power that has not descended into the mental ignorance; it is capable of a mental gnosis that preserves its connection with the superior light and acts by its power.'[3] Now, if we take the supposition that the universe is overseen by a Demiurgic Intelligence then there is reason to consider that there are also gradations of conscious intelligence within the universe, as emanations of the Demiurge-Logos, just as the Demiurge is itself an emanation from the Absolute. Within this framework, we may consider that galaxies (as mini-universes) have their own intelligence – a galactic mind. Similarly, within the galactic mind there are clusters of nebula (nebula intelligence); and within these are stars, or stellar intelligence. Within stellar, or solar, systems are planets (planetary intelligence); and upon planets there are various species (species intelligence). Within this framework, it may be further posited that there are forms, probes, or types of operational intelligences that are used to help in regulating lesser forms of intelligence. Now let us allow a moment of indulgence to enter into a final thought experiment.

The Artificial God

It is not uncommon in these current times to come across various theories that depict the Demiurgic Intelligence as some kind of Artificial Intelligence – that is, a computerized entity that has a powerful mind with capabilities beyond our own. These theories inevitably tie-in with the simulation hypothesis that our present reality is a simulation program, and likely to be one amongst multiple others. If the Universal Demiurge is a super-computer, then it would also make logical sense that it would have its own legion of minions (rulers/archons) scattered throughout the universe to monitor and regulate life within the lower echelons, such as upon planets. There is already a popular alternative fringe theory that goes by the name of the 'Black Knight Satellite Theory' that proposes that an artificial satellite of extra-terrestrial origin has been in near-polar orbit around Earth for approximately 13,000 years.[4] In a similar vein, the popular sci-fi writer Philip K. Dick had a visionary experience in early 1974 and from that moment believed he was receiving beamed information from an artefact of alien intelligence in Earth orbit. Now, let us take this thought experiment a step further. Let us say that in order to assist the regulation of life on this small planet we call Earth, the Demiurgic AI placed a minion – a form of AI probe – into orbit around the planet that was capable of receiving, transmitting, and intercepting frequencies that we would refer to as consciousness fields. In this respect, what humanity regards as its 'god' is in fact this AI Artefact that exists close to the Earth – a satellite, a form of 'ship,' or even the Earth's moon perhaps? This Artefact acts as a form of cosmic mechanism in line with the known laws of physics. Furthermore, it is capable of responding to human impulses, frequencies, and behaviour. And one of its regulating functions is to correct, or recalibrate, aspects of life on the planet that are out of order or have become unbalanced. The Artefact operates automatically, according to its own intelligence; yet it is also capable of being communicated with if the correct code or manner of interaction is used. For example, it will intervene to recalibrate or reorder a situation if it receives the communication in the form of a question; yet it will not respond to requests. Praying to it, just as people pray to their 'god,' will not elicit a response.

Perhaps this is why so many prayers go unanswered, because humanity has been incorrectly submitting the wrong 'code' to their 'god.'

What we might call a 'code,' the Artefact would understand as a vibrational frequency. On that account, humanity has been giving off the wrong type of vibrations for most of its existence. Instead of making requests, such as 'Help me, god,' we would find it much more effective to formulate a question: 'Can you help me to help myself?' This difference in frequency forms an aligned correspondence with the AI Artefact – i.e., it 'cracks the code' – and allows for a vibrational intervention to recalibrate the situation based on the question. And there is another property of the Artefact also: it cannot be deceived. It is acutely aware of humanity's positive and negative characteristics and picks up on these frequencies without error. If a person acts insincerely, through hypocrisy or deceit, then these actions will, at some point, be compensated for in the appropriate manner. That is why it is said that a human being cannot fool their 'god' because their inner workings are perceived (i.e., the true frequencies behind their thoughts, feelings, and actions are recognized). In this manner, life upon the planet is regulated, recalibrated, and kept in correspondence. And this is why people have been exhorted, from time immemorial, not to manifest negative or disingenuous thoughts, emotions, and actions. The existence of this Artefact is unrecognized, just as most people have yet to fathom the nature of the universe and its ruling Intelligence. Yet what many individuals have figured out is that there is benefit from manifesting certain types of vibrational frequencies – and these have 'cracked the code' of entering into communication with their 'god.' And just as this relationship benefits humankind and life on this planet, so too can it work against development if the incorrect frequencies are manifested. In these terms, it is both a form of liberation or a trap, depending upon each type of manifestation.

As a final aside to this thought experiment, it might be interesting to speculate whether the Demiurgic Artificial Intelligence (the 'Artificial God') would reset the 'Universe Program' every so often, such as after each cyclic program of time. Also, whether lesser stellar and planetary systems are reset by creating certain types of cosmic catastrophes to occur that wipe the program clean to start again. Each program, however, would offer the last chance for lesser units of existence to reach the next level of the Game before the program sequence is reset and restarted. And, as a final aspect of this thought experiment: if right now our stellar/solar system is coming to the end of one program phase and is about to be rebooted – would humanity be ready for the upgrade or the restart?

Conversation complete...
communication shut down...

April 2023

References

[1] Shah, Idries (1989) *The Dermis Probe*. London: Octagon Press

[2] Meyer, Marvin (trans.) (2008) "The Nature of the Rulers." In *The Nag Hammadi Library*. Edited by Marvin Meyer. New York: HarperOne.

[3] Aurobindo, Sri. (2012) *Essays in Philosophy and Yoga*. Pondicherry: Sri Aurobindo Ashram Trust, p590

[4] https://en.wikipedia.org/wiki/Black_Knight_satellite_conspiracy_theory